TRADING PLACES

STEVE WYATT
TRADING PLACES

ALLOWING GOD TO RENOVATE YOUR LIFE

Standard
PUBLISHING
Bringing The Word to Life™
Cincinnati, Ohio

Text © 2006 Steve Wyatt

Look for the *Trading Places* Group Participant's Guide, coming soon, ISBN 0-7847-1959-4

Printed in United States of America
Jacket & interior design: The DesignWorks Group; cover, David Uttley; interior, Robin Black
www.thedesignworksgroup.com
Edited by Diane Stortz and Lynn Lusby Pratt

ISBN 0-7847-1840-7

Library of Congress Cataloging-in-Publication Data

Wyatt, Steve, 1955-
  Trading places : allowing God to renovate your life / Steve Wyatt.
    p. cm.
  ISBN 0-7847-1840-7 (hardcover) -- ISBN 0-7847-7249-5 (softcover)
  1. Conversion—Christianity. 2. Christian life. 3. Bible—Biography. I. Title.

        BV4921.3.W93 2006
        248.2'4—dc22

2005023070
12 11 10 09 08 07 06   9 8 7 6 5 4 3 2 1

DEDICATION

To the One who walks in when all others walk away,
Who accepts me as I am, yet gently urges me toward what I can be.
To my Savior, Jesus:
You took my place.
You traded "no sin" to "be sin"—for me.
My feeble thank-you is my very life.
I purpose to live each day, Lord, exclusively for You.

ACKNOWLEDGEMENTS

ANY MAJOR PROJECT REQUIRES a team effort, and this is no exception.

I still can't believe I made such a reckless decision, but I started this book the same week we launched a new church in Anthem, Arizona, called Christ's Church at The Crossroads.

What a crazy ride it's been! And for that, I need (once again) to ask forgiveness from Cindy and our sizable brood. You had no idea what it would be like when you said, "Go for it!" but how supportive and faithful you have been! Thank you.

To The Crossroads church family, for the many times you needed me and I wasn't there, yet you freely offered grace, thank you.

To Rachel Brand for your research and Phil Kinney for your many creative contributions, thanks. The ink that adorns these pages is because we, too, forged a partnership.

CONTENTS

INTRODUCTION

WHEN I FIRST LEARNED TO RIDE a two-wheeler, the bike I rode was a brand sparkling new, cherry red Schwinn Roadmaster, complete with chrome, red and white streamers, a mirror on the handlebars, and genuine imitation leather saddlebags on the side.

We lived in Covington, Virginia, at the time, and our home on Fudge Street was the place to be . . . in the winter. We lived on a very steep hill, and everyone came to Fudge Street to go sledding.

But in the spring, Fudge Street was the pits for riding bikes, especially for rookie riders like me. In fact, the only place I could learn to ride was in the alley right beside our home.

The alley was flat—and that was good.

But the alley was also gravel—and that was bad.

Looking out across that stretch of jagged rock, I knew that if I took a tumble, I'd be hamburger. But I was determined to learn to ride, so I took off.

I did pretty well at first, but then, when I realized what I was doing—much like Peter must have felt when he walked on the water—I panicked. My front wheel started wobbling, my body stiffened in fear. I yelled . . . and then I fell!

Hot tears flooded my eyes as I quickly assessed the damage. The good news? My bike was OK. The bad news? I wasn't. My palms were scraped and stung like crazy. My knees were bleeding; my pants were torn. But worst of all, my ego really took a hit! I had failed at the one thing every boy is supposed to do instinctively!

Then, almost in spite of myself, like the fabled phoenix, I rose from the ashes of my defeat and picked up my bike. With eyes set like steel, I thought, *Alley, you can't have me! I'm gonna beat you. I'm gonna learn to ride this bike—no matter how many times I fall!*

My failure became, for me, a defining moment. Would I give up, or would I plow ahead? Would I lie in the dust in anguish over my defeat, or would I pick myself up and stay at the task?

I mounted and prepared for round two.

And this time I took off and never looked back.

I share this story because I really believe that life's most defining moments take place at just such a crossroads. It's when we find ourselves parked at the corner of Defeat and Despair, it's while languishing in the backwash of some embarrassing failure, that we take a gut check and ask:

Am I going to wave the white flag and surrender? Or am I going to muster my courage and forge on?

Am I content to wallow in this humiliating, hurting place?

Will this moment of shame be the final chapter of my life? Or is there another sequel, yet unwritten?

What a loss to our world when we decide to put down the pen and walk away. What a great joy when we who know disappointment and heartache decide that the pain is too great to stay in that painful place.

How wonderful that moment when our heart finally gets the point of the "alley" and understands that God gave us our story— so how can we do anything other than freely tell it?

Mustering the courage to make a change is hard.

It's one thing to summon the strength to climb back on your bike—it's another thing, entirely, to climb back into your life.

It's risky. The path is not always so clearly marked. But the alternative is a dark passageway leading nowhere.

This book is about making a change that will last. But please understand—courage alone won't sustain lasting change. True life change is a renovation only God can pull off.

He wants to pull it off—in partnership with you.

And that . . . is what Trading Places is all about.

PART ONE

THE GREAT EXCHANGE

Replacing my weakness with God's strength
When faced with the need to make a change, the first and most important step we need to take is to make the Great Exchange. We've got to Trade Places with God and allow Him to replace our weakness with His strength.

PUTTING OFF AND PUTTING ON

The essential response
Receiving new strength is not the end of our renovation. No, we've got to use that new strength to add some new items to our spiritual wardrobes. That's where Putting Off and Putting On comes in.

THE *X* FACTOR

How real change happens
God doesn't just zap people . . . lasting change is a partnership. God has a part to play, but so do we. What's our part? Well, that's the *X* Factor.

CHAPTER 1

THE GREAT EXCHANGE

THIS BOOK IS CALLED *Trading Places,* and it's all about making a change that will last.

It also sounds strikingly similar to one very hot cable television show.

Now since it's just you and me huddled under your favorite reading light, are you willing to admit that you've watched at least one episode of that cult-phenom, *Trading Spaces?* If so, you probably think *Trading Places* is a takeoff—maybe even a *rip*-off—of that show.

If you've never seen *Trading Spaces,* the premise is simple: neighbors get a once-in-a-lifetime chance to do a massive makeover in one room of each other's home. They get two days and a thousand bucks, along with the services of a self-proclaimed decorator and a self-admiring carpenter.

Each hour-long episode follows the progress of these homegrown do-overs, culminating in "the reveal," that magical moment when the neighbors, eyes securely covered, are led into their respective homes by that way-too-perky Paige Davis, and they're allowed—*ta-da!*—to see . . . how do I put this? . . . the interesting results.

To me, the show's best moment is when the camera moves in for a close-up and the homeowners uncover their eyes and start shouting, "Ohmygod! Ohmygod! Ohmygod!" And we get to decipher whether that "Ohmygod!" means they're delighted or ticked, thrilled beyond words or suffering an aneurysm. My guess is, more often than not, they're just trying not to throw up!

I suppose it's possible to pick up some helpful, cheap decorating tips from *Trading Spaces*, but people don't watch the show to get ideas; they watch hoping this week's project will completely unravel—that the designer will totally weird out and slap lime green paint on the walls, wallpaper the living room with hay, and dress up the fireplace with dancing pink flamingos! Because once the hay starts flying? Veteran *Trading Spaces* fans all know there's going to be blood at the reveal.

Which is why all participants are told beforehand there's a real good chance they won't like the final product. In fact, all applicants for the show are required to sign a release acknowledging that *Trading Spaces* is not responsible, in any way, for redoing their room gone bad.

CHANGE IS RISKY

Which brings us to the topic of change. When you've decided that you want or even *need* to make a change in your life, doing it the *Trading Spaces* way is risky business. Really risky. Because invariably, to make the change, you have to release something—just like the show's participants release a room in their homes. But you release it, believing the trade will be worth it.

Now it wouldn't be risky if you were guaranteed that everything you release is going be replaced by something even better. But that's not *Trading Spaces*—and that's not real life, either.

In the show, each participant gets to cull his or her room for family artifacts and irreplaceable keepsakes to protect them from the makeover. They even get the chance to replace the actual room's furniture with some of the rattiest stuff they own, and they can coach their counterparts about color schemes that would be entirely *un*acceptable. In other words, they still have a degree of ownership in the change.

What we'll discover as we move through this book, however, is that when you decide to make a change *in your life,* you have to remove yourself *entirely* from the driver's seat—you have to relinquish your death grip on whatever it is you deeply care about and then leave the final results entirely in the hands of another . . . in the hands of God.

Please understand: trying to make a lasting renovation in your life by Trading Spaces (you let go, but only after some carefully negotiated limitations and selfishly driven directives) is a bad trade . . . a really bad trade. Primarily because the Trading Spaces way still allows you to make changes according to *your* rules.

But who's to say that you know what trade is actually in your best interest?

Consider Michael Phelps, the golden boy of the 2004 Summer Olympic Games. Phelps took home a record eight medals. He became an overnight hero and enjoyed a personal marketability worth millions. But now, according to his manager, his image has been "shattered." You see, Phelps was arrested just four months later for driving under the influence. As one radio announcer put it, "It seems that the great Olympian Michael Phelps can not only swim like a fish, he evidently drinks like one, too."

Bad trade, Michael. Trading your impeccable and extremely marketable image for one lousy buzz? That's Trading Spaces—making a change, but with *my* hand still on the wheel. Which is why Michael's manager is openly wondering if Michael's image can be salvaged.[1]

Scott Peterson wanted to make a change, too. He wanted freedom, so he traded his pregnant wife and unborn son for a death sentence.

Bad trade, Scottie.

The Boston Red Sox wanted to change their post-season misfortunes, so they traded Babe Ruth to the Yankees and received in exchange a curse that lasted almost a century.

In 1626, Indians traded the island of Manhattan for $24 worth of beads and trinkets. Richard Nixon, seeking reelection, traded secrecy for disgrace and a presidential resignation.

Martha Stewart, wanting to make a fast buck, traded insider information for a five-month stay in prison.

Bill Clinton traded momentary pleasure for impeachment.

It's true: making a change is risky business. Especially when you make the change and insist on doing so by your rules. When change is made that way? The change doesn't work out so well.

Is Trading Places Realistic?

Now I know you realize that this book is not about a redecorating show. It's not a takeoff, either. It's actually a throwback. All the way back to 1983 and a movie called—are you with me?—*Trading Places*.

The movie stars Eddie Murphy as Billy Ray Valentine, a down-on-his-luck street hustler, and Dan Aykroyd as Louis Winthorpe III, a successful New York commodities broker.

Now socialists have debated for years the impact of environment versus genetics. Is it nature that determines the kind of person we will be, or is it nurture? Well, in the movie two elderly millionaires make a wager on that very point. Randolph Duke believes he can take a common criminal and make him a successful businessman—*and* that he can remove Louis from his riches and he'll become a criminal.

Mortimer Duke disagrees, so for their usual one-dollar bet, the whole plan for change is set in motion.

By the way, you may recognize this plot. It's essentially the same conversation that took place between Satan and the Lord regarding Job. Satan believed that Job was good only because his environment was good. Take away all that good stuff, Satan claimed, and Job would become just as vile as the rest of his fellow men.

So that's the bet.

At first glance, the movie seems to suggest that Randolph was right. Billy really takes to the business (not to mention all those new toys), and Louis nearly commits a heinous crime before they both realize they've been duped. That's when both young men join forces to teach the Duke brothers a lesson.

By movie's end, the theory has been disproved, as the movie's most blessed duo, those conniving Duke brothers, turns out to be the most depraved—living in the lap of luxury yet betting on two men's misfortunes for nothing more than one lousy dollar and the satisfaction of being right.

Then again, Billy and Louis also mess up. They aren't content just to settle the score—they want to destroy those Dukes. And in the final scene, with a series of trading maneuvers that economists still puzzle over today, *Billy Ray and Louis actually pull it off!*

Now what Billy Ray and Louis do in the last scene of the movie isn't even possible in real life—only in the make-believe world of Hollyweird. But in attempting to pull it off, they do exactly what our friends on the *Trading Spaces* show do. They try to make a change—but by *their* rules.

So the bottom line: even though the movie is called *Trading Places*—nobody really does. Billy is still a hustler, Louis is still trapped by his greed, and the Duke boys are still playing games. Each wanted to make a change—but they wanted to do it their way.

Which brings me to a second lesson about making a change. *Change is hard.* And true, lasting change? Seldom works the way you'd think it would.

Consider the apostle Paul. Talk about needing to make a change. Paul had "a thorn in [his] flesh" and living with that thorn, in his own words, was "torment" (2 Corinthians 12:7). Some say the "thorn" was epilepsy, or malaria, or maybe migraine headaches. Others claim it was an estranged wife or a chronic eye disease. Whatever it was, Paul wanted it gone! He said, "Three times I pleaded with the Lord to take it away" (v. 8).

But look at how God answered those pleas. He said, "My grace is sufficient for you, for my power is made perfect in weakness" (v. 9).

In other words, God said no.

"Paul, I'll take care of your thorn. Just know, the great need for change you face is not thorn removal, it's how you decide to respond to that thorn. So I'm not taking it away, nor am I suggesting that you can take this weakness and turn it into a strength. What I want you to discover is this: my power is made perfect in your weakness. When you're at your weakest moment, that's when I am strong. So instead of taking the thorn away, I'm going to give you the grace to endure it. As you tap into my grace, you'll watch my strength trade places with your thorn."

And that's exactly what happened. Paul wrote, "Therefore I will boast all the more gladly about my weaknesses, so that Christ's power may rest on me" (v. 9).

Now that's quite a change. Not exactly the change Paul was looking for, but still a change. Rather than continuing to beg God to remove the thorn, Paul received God's grace in order to embrace his thorn. And he learned how, in doing that, God's strength can trade places with our weakness.

That's what I call the Great Exchange.

THE GREAT EXCHANGE

Do you realize what Paul discovered in that encounter? He learned that problems cannot be solved at the same level they're created. Which means Trading Spaces doesn't work. I mean, release is an important part of the deal. But you can't just hand over your heartache to someone who also deals with heartache. That's no way to make lasting change.

And Paul also learned that true life change isn't sourced in nature or nurture, either. I mean, if making a change is only about *you* and the strength you alone can bring to that moment—trust me, when life gets tough, you'll fold faster than Louis Winthorpe III.

Because true change—change that lasts—is not about you! It's really not!

It's all about *where*. Where does your strength come from?

If lasting change is really all about making the Great Exchange— if it's all about finding Christ's power right in the vortex of my own weakness—the big question is this:

Exactly how do I do that?

Thorny Theology

Let's travel back to the ancient book of Isaiah. In chapter 40, the prophet mentions two reactions that are common to everyone in need of change. Maybe they're in torment, like Paul. Maybe it's a physical malady or a relationship disaster or a financial conundrum. But whatever it is, there is *no* discernible solution.

How do people typically react when faced with a thorny problem?

Look at Isaiah 40:27: "My way is hidden from the LORD." That's the first thing we think: God has flown the coop. And that's why Trading Spaces is such an attractive option. I mean, if God is missing, then I need to figure this out myself! If I can't see Him or feel Him or don't hear from Him—He must not be around. "My way is hidden!"

What's the second thing we think when surrounded by thorns? "My cause is disregarded" (v. 27). In other words, "God isn't interested in what I need. And since He obviously doesn't care about getting my life turned around? I'm going have to do it myself!"

But hold on. How does God respond to our typical reactions? "Do you not know? Have you not heard?" (v. 28).

Gee, *that* helps!

Have you ever been upset or impatient or just plain worn-out from the struggle, only to have someone say, "Don't you know?" or "Haven't you heard?" Why, that's the most comfortless counsel you can imagine. *Unless it's true.*

What Is God Like?

Isaiah 40 is a wonderful short course in the nature and awesome power of God, as the prophet reveals truths about God in rapid-fire delivery.

God is in control. God "has measured the waters in the hollow of his hand" and "with the breadth of his hand marked off the heavens" (v. 12). He has also "held the dust of the earth in a basket" and "weighed the mountains on the scales and the hills in a balance."

No mere man has ever done such things—only God.

In verse 13, the Lord asks, "Who has understood the mind of the LORD, or instructed him as his counselor?"

His intellect and wisdom are far beyond that of mortals.

"To whom, then, will you compare God?" (v. 18).

The answer is, no one.

Isaiah draws the only conclusion that can be drawn: "Do you not know? Have you not heard? Has it not been told you from the beginning? Have you not understood since the earth was founded? He sits enthroned above the circle of the earth" (vv. 21, 22).

Our God resides far above human conflict. He cares for us and sympathizes with us in our pain, but He's not shocked by the course of human events. He isn't getting an ulcer because of Iraq. He's not panicking because of the tsunami or Hurricane Katrina. He's not fretting about the moral decline of our culture.

He cares . . . but He is also in control.

God himself asks, "'To whom will you compare me? Or who is my equal?' . . . Lift your eyes and look to the heavens: Who created all these? He who brings out the starry host one by one, and calls them each by name. Because of His great power and mighty strength, not one of them is missing" (vv. 25, 26).

That's the theme of verse 28: Don't you know? Haven't you heard? Lift up your eyes! "The LORD is the everlasting God."

And because He is, this thing you think you need to change is well within the scope of His knowledge. He's the LORD, after all! And as Lord, He is over all and above all and in all. He is totally aware and absolutely in sync with whatever it is you're going through.

And since He reigns on high, He has the full panoramic view of your life—including all things past, present, and future! All you can see is your past and right now! And "right now" is thorny. It's a torment! You can't possibly imagine how God could use that thorn for good.

But from His perspective, God sees the whole spectrum of your life. And He says, "I know what I'm doing. I see what you're going through, and I can handle it. I'm not tired. I'm not freaked out. I'm not wondering, *What in the world am I going to do about that?* I'm not chewing Tums or taking Zoloft. I know in complete fullness the whole story of your life. And I know how it's going to turn out, because I'm in charge, remember?"

God is powerful and strong. Not only is God in control, He is also "the Creator of the ends of the earth" (v. 28). Which means He has *power* to handle whatever comes down your pike. And in case you're wondering about His energy level, "He will not grow tired or weary, and his understanding no one can fathom" (v. 28).

He's the creator of all things who understands absolutely everything. He is full of compassion and goodness. He will never do you wrong. He will never leave you in the lurch. He'll never turn His back on you when you need Him.

Now He may not move according your timetable, and He may, as with Paul, decide that it's better for to you live with your weakness in His strength than for Him to take that weakness away—but that's His call. Because He is, after all, everlasting!

And all that strength of His? "He gives strength to the weary and increases the power of the weak" (v. 29). Is that cool or what? God takes His enormous strength and He just gives it away—to "the weary." To the very people who *thought* they had enough strength, so they relied on that strength, but then ran out of gas. Who *thought* they could find their own way, but couldn't see so clearly after all and landed in even deeper weeds than where they started. To these poor, weary souls—you know, *you and me*—God gives strength.

And it's not just "If only I were a little younger!" Nah. "Even youths grow tired and weary, and young men stumble and fall"

(v. 30). I mean, like it or not, "stumble" is what we do, young or old!

So what do you do when "stumble" happens? When you've been grounded, and you're not sure where to turn—and not sure you've got the strength to go there even if you did know.

Do you hike down every possible rabbit trail? Race down each dead end, butting up against every obstacle, only to wind up bloody and tired and angry and frustrated? Is that what you do?

That's what *we* do. Just like an episode of *Trading Spaces*. Gotta get the project done. Make the final touches. Get the room together. Hurry, hurry, hurry!

"Yet those who wait for the LORD will gain new strength; they will mount up with wings like eagles, they will run and not get tired, they will walk and not become weary" (v. 31, NASB). That's the Great Exchange: my weakness for God's strength. Trading *Places*.

And the key to completing this transaction? Don't charge ahead and do it yourself! Don't think that a thousand bucks and two days are going to help. Don't think that somehow you're going to pull this off in your own strength. Because that kind of change will never last. To find true, lasting change you've got to make God's Great Exchange.

And His promise of unbridled, undiminished, unequaled strength is freely reserved . . . for those who "wait."

FOR THOSE WHO WAIT

Not those who rush ahead, or finagle their way through, or scramble and scratch till they've got an ulcer, a migraine, high blood pressure, and two strokes. Those who *wait*.

The Hebrew word translated *wait* means to twist or stretch in order to make something strong. As a noun, it means "rope," and it carries the idea of stretching or twisting a little strand of hair around other little strands of hair, and then that group of strands is wrapped around another group of strands, until finally a massive rope is formed. So that the original strand—now wrapped within the interior of what is now a thick rope—becomes as strong as the rope itself.

Those who wait for the Lord, Isaiah 40:31 is saying—those who are willing to Trade Places and by faith allow God to wrap His power around their measly little strand of weakness—those who wait will receive in exchange four amazing benefits.

New Strength

The first benefit that you receive in exchange for your weakness is *new strength.*

When you decide to trust God enough that you put your hope in His strength and not yours—when you decide to hit the brakes, stick it in neutral, and place your ultimate confidence in Him—when you decide that your need isn't going to be resolved by pasting pink flamingos on fireplaces—He's going to reward that faith by infusing your life with new strength.

No longer will you come to the end of the day exhausted. No longer will you fall into bed dog-tired because you've spent all your energy trying to work yourself out of a jam—trying to make a trade, plug the holes, get it right.

And though people all around you may be collapsing from exhaustion, God will bring to you who wait for Him a strength you could never know apart from Him. That's the Great Exchange.

Did you know that when a storm approaches, an eagle doesn't fly away from that storm? He actually flies *into* the storm. Because the eagle knows that if he sets his wings to the wind, with hardly any effort at all he can catch those powerful updrafts and fly higher and faster and stronger *because of the storm* than he could ever fly on his own.

And so can you. That's why God seldom just takes away weakness. He knows that with His strength wrapped around your weakness, your weakness will cause you to fly higher and longer and stronger than you could ever fly without it.

So set your face to the wind. Put your trust in God—and "wait." He will give you new strength.

A Better Perspective

The second benefit of Trading Places is that you gain *a better perspective.*

Isaiah says, "They will soar on wings like eagles." The beauty of soaring is not just the freedom you feel. No, when you're as high as an eagle can fly, you can see a lot farther ahead.

I'm told that on a clear day an eagle can spot a fish in a lake several miles away. And you will see with unusual clarity, too, when you learn to wait. Not only do you gain new strength, you mount up with wings and you soar! And as you soar, you develop the ability to see life differently than when you were just walking.

Now you can see out into the future, you can see through painful circumstances, you can see the path that God is laying out before you. You can see His perfect plan unfolding right before your eyes.

Increased Stamina

The third benefit of Trading Places is *increased stamina.* You "will run and not grow weary."

You're not getting weary because you aren't pressing anymore. No longer are you frantically devising exit strategies and wringing your hands in fear and wracking your brain for an answer and pacing the floor in panic. Instead, you just let God wrap His enormous power around your measly little strand of rope—and you wait.

You don't work late into the night; you rest! I don't mean you do nothing. It's just that what you do brings results, and results keep your heart from growing weary.

Bob Ringewold was driving when—*BOOM!*—he looked up and saw the caved-in roof of his car. He stopped and got out to find that an eight-pound sucker fish had just fallen from the sky and smashed his car! Evidently the fish had fallen from the talons of an eagle that couldn't hold on anymore.

You know what Ringewold did? This is so cool. He took the fish home and fried it up for dinner.

Now I don't know Ringewold from a ringworm—but I know this: Ringewold's been through some stuff. And I know that because he took a hit, but he kept moving anyway. I mean, the dude hardly missed a beat!

That's what happens when you learn to wait. You become so strong in Him that setbacks no longer hold you back! Instead, whenever life drops a salmon on you? You make salmon-ade! (Sorry.)

So if your home is filled with prickly, gnarly thorns right now, don't just Trade Spaces and frantically try, in your own power, to redecorate your life! Instead, Trade *Places* and let God redo your life in a wonderfully creative and absolutely stunning thorn theme that, in time, will absolutely transform you!

Because that's what the Great Exchange is all about.

A Stronger Resistance

There's a fourth benefit to Trading Places. You *strengthen your resistance* to future obstacles. You find that you can "walk [*and walk and walk*] and not become weary."

You don't "become weary" because throughout this whole ordeal you've been letting God wrap His big rope around your little strand. You've been feeding on His strength and seeing things from His perspective and storing up all kinds of extra resolve.

And He's been putting steel in your frame and speaking encouragement to your heart.

Part of our problem is we think that waiting means nothing is happening. But don't you believe it.

Because the truth is, God is at work in those unseen corridors of your life, and He's building within you a strength that will not be denied. That's why I'm telling you: whatever doesn't beat you down will build you up! And make you stronger for the next time a fish lands on your car.

It Didn't Come to Stay . . .

A friend wrote me a note sometime ago. And talk about going through stuff? This woman has a lifetime supply of salmon-ade! In her note to me, she said that one of her favorite phrases in the Bible is "And it came to pass."

It didn't come to stay . . . it came to pass.

Whatever is in your life right now? It hasn't come to stay. It came to pass.

This thorn you're dealing with won't be with you forever. It didn't come to stay. It came to pass. It did!

But in the meantime? Before it fully passes? You've got to wait.

Isaiah 40:31 speaks to three inescapable stages of life. There are times when life is like an eagle's. You just set your wings to the wind and you fly! Life is good and God is great.

But there are other times when life isn't so exciting. Oh, you're making it. You're running, but you're certainly not tip-toeing through tulips. At best, you're just getting by.

There are still other times when all you can do is remind yourself to breathe. You're just trying to hold on.

Isaiah tells us that even then, we've got to wait. Because our God does His best work in dark times. He's not going to leave you in the lurch. He's not going to walk away. No, He'll make the very trade you need. When the time is right, He'll carry you on His wings to some new, high place—and you will be forever and eternally changed.

See, Trading Places, unlike Trading Spaces, isn't risky at all. If your trading partner is God, you're tapping into not only His power but also His character! And remember, our God is not just a mighty God; our God's word is true!

And that's vital, because making a change is not about the size of your faith or the level of your effort! It's in whom you have placed your trust. Place it in yourself—or your neighbor—and you'll wind up in a room filled with hay and pink flamingos. But place your trust in the Lord and wait for Him to do what He alone can do, and you'll soar like an eagle.

Stop Working, Start Waiting

My wife and I are spending time with a young woman who is right now in the throes of a Trading Places dilemma. She's deep in debt and has also become seriously involved with a young man who really cares about her.

The trouble is, the financial deal is eating her alive! She's trying to manage, but you know how it is—there's got to be an easier way, right?

So you know what they've come up with? "Let's move in together. That way we can halve our expenses and get out of debt faster. And we can find out if we're right for each other and whether, in fact, we belong together. This makes perfect sense!"

Truth is, that plan is just Trading Spaces. It's moving from one location to another, but haulin' all her stinkin' garbage right along behind her. It's a two-day plan that could ruin the rest of her life.

If my young friend goes ahead with this plan, she will live to regret it. Trading Spaces is nothing more than rearranging deck chairs on the *Titanic*! It doesn't change a thing, and it keeps you from doing what really could change things!

How much better to just Trade Places. To move off the throne of your life and let God sit there instead. To stop frantically pacing and strategizing and actualizing your latest, greatest escape plan—and instead, just wait on Him.

That's what my young friend should do. She needs to slow way, way down and spend some time letting God wrap His rope of strength aroung her little strand. She needs to let God be God, and freely admit that she is not.

And if she'll do that? God will transform all her weaknesses into enormous strength, and a change will take place in her—a change quite unlike any change she could even begin to imagine, a change for her good. That's the way it works when you stop Trading Spaces and decide to Trade Places.

Please take a close look at these words. The Bible says, "Since before time began no one has ever imagined, no ear heard, no eye seen, a God like you who works for those who wait for him. You meet those who happily do what is right, who keep a good memory of the way you work" (Isaiah 64:4, 5, THE MESSAGE).

God moves in direct response, He acts on my behalf, He works for my cause—when I do what? *When I wait for Him*, when I get my weakness wrapped up by His strength, when I put my trust in Him and not in myself or anybody else. God goes to work in the very moment I *stop* working—when I stop Trading Spaces and finally decide to Trade Places.

CHAPTER 2

PUTTING OFF AND PUTTING ON

WHILE WE'RE ON THE TOPIC of cable TV shows, do you remember a rather quirky, short-lived show on the E! channel called *Fashion Emergency?*

I do. But the only reason I do is because my daughter loved to watch it. So please don't question my manhood.

Anyway, *Fashion Emergency* was based on a simple premise: common, everyday people—tired of their outdated wardrobes, embarrassed by their do-nothing hair or frustrated by those ratty jeans their boyfriends always wear—were encouraged to write the show and say, "Help! I've got a Fashion Emergency! I need a makeover!"

Usually, there was a class reunion coming up, or a wedding they were invited to—and they really wanted to look their best. Actually, they wanted to look *better* than their best.

So they called. Not the Ghostbusters . . . they called E! And if they got picked? The Fashion Emergency First Response Team kicked into gear and the action got intense!

They started by shopping at an exclusive boutique (not a department store, certainly not Wal-Mart), and they picked a wardrobe worth about one-tenth of what they actually paid for it.

Then they got their hair done, usually at a *sal*on. Not a sa*lon* . . . and definitely not a sa*loon*—at a *sal*on.

Then there was makeup and shoes and other accessories until finally the contestant headed out to his or her big night—perfectly polished, groomed, combed, and *extremely confident.*

Then as the credits rolled and the show drew to a close, the happy recipient of this new look tearfully thanked all the good folks at the E! channel for helping avert yet another—*da-da-da!* Fashion Emergency!

I know what you're thinking: *what* does a silly show like that have to do with something as serious as Trading Places?

I'm glad you asked.

As we saw in chapter one, when faced with the need to make a change, the first and most important step is to make the Great Exchange. And the Great Exchange takes place when we "wait on the Lord," right? When we let God *be* God, and instead of continually and frantically and foolishly Trading Spaces (which is nothing more than moving from one painful space to another painful space, only to realize we're still dragging behind us the same baggage we thought we were leaving), we decide, instead, to Trade *Places.*

So what's the primary action step in Trading Places?

Wait.

But wait!

Sorry.

To wait doesn't mean to do nothing. The truth is, as we "wait on the Lord," God uses what we consider downtime to build within us new strength. Even more, this brief hiatus provides us with a new perspective on life. And it builds within us a greater stamina for the journey ahead and, even more, a strong resistance to future obstacles.

Here's some good news: all this new strength God provides is far more effective than steroids, and you don't have to worry about random drug tests.

But what are we supposed to do with all this new strength? I've got more stamina now and I'm stronger than I've ever been before, so what do I do with all this newfound power? Do I have all this new spiritual muscle just so I can flex it and impress people with how buff I am?

Of course not! No, after you make the Great Exchange, there's a second response that's needed. And it's just as essential as the first.

PUTTING OFF AND PUTTING ON

It's called Putting Off and Putting On. Paul introduces the idea in Ephesians 4:22-24. The image is one of putting on and putting off articles of clothing. That's where *Fashion Emergency* comes in.

Scripture often illustrates the need for change by describing a change in clothing. For example, in Romans 13 Paul reminds believers that Christ is coming again and that "the day is almost here. So let us put aside the deeds of darkness and put on the armor of light" (v. 12).

Put aside . . . put on. And in case we still don't get it, Paul adds, "Clothe yourselves with the Lord Jesus Christ, and do not think about how to gratify the desires of the sinful nature" (v. 14).

In Ephesians, he says, "Put on the full armor of God" (6:13).

Jesus said, "Be dressed ready for service and keep your lamps burning" (Luke 12:35). I like that. He promised His disciples that He'd send the Holy Spirit, and then He added, "But stay in the city until you have been clothed with power from on high" (Luke 24:49).

My favorite "fashion emergency" verse is Colossians 3:12: "Therefore, as God's chosen people, holy and dearly loved, clothe yourselves with compassion, kindness, humility, gentleness and patience."

So when Paul, in Ephesians 4, tells us to Put Off and Put On various articles of spiritual clothing, what he's saying is: receiving new strength isn't the end of the story. No, you've got to *use* that strength to add some new items to your spiritual wardrobe.

And no, by "spiritual wardrobe" I *don't* have in mind cheap T-shirts, WWJD bracelets, and huge, garish wooden crosses. I'm talking about God's plan for doing a huge makeover in your life from the inside out.

In Ephesians 4, the whole idea Paul is driving at is that if you actually Trade Places—come to that moment when you let God be God and admit that you *aren't* God—then, on the basis of that trade, you're going to look different than you used to. You're going to look like God.

"So I tell you this, and insist on it in the Lord, that you must no longer live as the Gentiles do" (v. 17).

Now relax, because the description we're about to read is an obvious generalization. Then again, it's also the truth.

Walking Like a Gentile

In Paul's day, you either lived for God or you lived like a Gentile. It's just the way the distinction was made. *Gentile* was the term used to describe an ordinary, garden-variety, you've-seen-one-you've-seen-them-all unbeliever. So Paul is saying, "If you've made the Great Exchange—and you're a believer—why are you living like an unbeliever?"

Exactly how does an unbeliever live?

Well, "in the futility of their [own] thinking" (Ephesians 4:17). You know . . . where making life work is all up to me. I've got to connect the dots, I've got to make things happen, because God is missing, remember?

Even more, unbelievers are also "darkened in their understanding and separated from the life of God because of the ignorance that is in them due to the hardening of their hearts" (v. 18). Now Paul's not being cruel; that's the way it is. You live as a Gentile, and you will—do you see the downward spiral?— become fuzzy in your thinking, which negatively impacts your ability to process the truth. And in this darkened condition, your heart gets calloused and hard. And that's when the fuses really blow: "Having lost all sensitivity, they have given themselves over to sensuality so as to indulge in every kind of impurity, with a continual lust for more" (v. 19).

Sounds like Paul's getting a little overheated! As he talks about hard hearts and futile thinking and unbridled sensuality, you get the sense the ol' ticker is really racing as all kinds of emotions percolate within.

Part of that emotion, I'm convinced, is a reflection of his own inconsistencies—times when, just like us, Paul looked like a Gentile.

Dressing Like a Christian

Which is why, with great emotion, Paul says, "You, however, did not come to know Christ that way" (v. 20). In other words, "That's not the way a believer is taught to dress. Christians don't wear stuff like that. I mean, it's one thing for the world to look like that, but not you! You've made the Great Exchange. You're cut from a different bolt of cloth. You're not supposed to look like Gentiles; you're supposed to look like Jesus!"

"Surely you heard of him and were taught in him in accordance with the truth that is in Jesus" (v. 21). Paul is asking, "What I'm saying here is ringing some bells, right? I mean, you were taught this stuff, weren't you?"

"You were taught, with regard to your former way of life, to put off your old self, which is being corrupted by its deceitful desires; to be made new in the attitude of your minds; and to put on the new self, created to be like God in true righteousness and holiness" (vv. 22-24).

You got that message, right? Because that's how you're supposed to dress. That's the fashion statement a true Christ-follower makes. You're a Christian, right? So dress like one! Dress in such a way that you look just "like God"!

Remember *The Waltons?* John-Boy was leaving home and going to college. So the entire clan gathered to send him off.

But his father, every time he tried to say good-bye, was either interrupted or he'd get so choked up he couldn't speak.

Finally, as he and John-Boy rode alone to the train station, he looked his son in the eye and said, "John-Boy, you remember who you are."

That's pretty much all he said. Yet he communicated more in those six words than an hour's lecture could have accomplished. "John-Boy, you've been raised right. You've got a good moral base and a strong set of values. You're the firstborn son, the model for the rest of our family. So, son, remember who you are."

That's Paul message to us. He says in verse 17, "You must no longer live as the Gentiles." In other words, stop adjusting your lifestyle to fit the culture! Why? Because you're created, verse 24 says, "to be like God," that's why.

Isn't it amazing how powerfully fashion dictates our lives? Wide ties are in, next fall they're out. One month it's short hair, next month it's long. As I'm writing, it's all about pointy shoes and UnderArmour and Roxy T-shirts. But about the time you get that stuff? There's a whole new list of stuff!

And we're all victims of this fashion craze, but teenagers are like lemmings marching right into the sea—except they march into Gap and Hollister. And if I even try to suggest that my kids go anywhere else? "I don't think so, Dad!" Like mindless drones, they wear whatever peer pressure tells them to wear.

My daughter bought a ball cap from American Eagle for $25. But it already had a hole in it, threads ripped out and hanging in her face! She brought it to the cash register, and I said, "Jessie! Go get another cap! That one's torn up!" She looked at me— well, you know how she looked at me—and rolled her eyes and said, "Dad! It's supposed to be this way!"

But Paul says, "Believers, you're *not* supposed to be this way. Just because the Gentiles do these things doesn't mean you should. You need to remember who you are and dress accordingly. Stop adapting to the style of our culture, and instead, do your best to look like God."

GOD'S MAKEOVER PLAN

How do I do that? I mean, what kind of makeover does God want for me, anyway?

That's the right way to ask the question, because this is God's makeover plan, right? Not yours.

I came across an interesting ad for software that allows you to enter your measurements, hair color, and basic skin type in order to create a 3D model of you. The ad says, "This is the most exciting new way to experiment with your look! It's easy to use. One click and you're a blonde, a redhead, or a brunette.

Feeling adventurous? Then change your hairstyle or reshape your lips and brows. You can even change the color of your eyes . . . right on the computer! Thousands of new looks are just a click away!"

The only problem is, the makeover Paul's talking about is about the look *God* wants—not what you may want. He says in Ephesians 4:24 you've "put on the new self"; you've been "created to be like God." So this makeover is about reflecting Him. It's about looking as much like Him as you can. Romans 8:29 says that God has predetermined every believer should "be conformed to the likeness of his Son."

So what does God look like? In the verses that follow, Paul mentions five wardrobe accessories that the devoted Christian Puts Off and then what he Puts On instead. These are accessories complementing the overall look. The foundation of your basic wardrobe and of this new you is Christ.

Truth, Not Falsehood

The first item Paul mentions is truth. A true Christ follower will Put Off falsehood and Put On the truth. "Each of you must put off falsehood and speak truthfully to his neighbor, for we are all members of one body" (Ephesians 4:25).

The typical Gentile, Paul says, practices speaking behaviors that play havoc with the truth. And yes, that *is* a broad generalization. But that doesn't mean it isn't also the way it is.

I heard about a judge in Kentucky who came home at 5:30 one morning. His wife said, "Where have you been?"

"Well, the light was off when I got home last night at midnight. I didn't want to disturb you, so I slept on the porch swing."

She said, "I had that porch swing taken down a month ago."

He said, "That's my story, and I'm sticking to it."

That's the Gentile way. Our culture is shot through with dishonesty. We lie on income tax returns, we fake Medicare forms, we lie about our weight and age. But most of all, we lie to get out of trouble.

And while it's true that a lie is an abomination before God (Proverbs 6:16, 17, KJV), it's also a very present help in times of trouble!

So it's true, the Gentile has in his wardrobe lots and lots of falsehood.

Remember when Jesus confronted some folks about their deception? He said, in effect, "I need to say something, but you won't want to hear it. Those lies you tell? The deceit you're involved in? It's happening because you're connected to the father of lies." John 8:44 tells us Jesus said, "You belong to your father, the devil . . . [and] there is no truth in him. When he lies, he speaks his native language, for he is a liar and the father of lies."

But Paul is telling the Ephesians, "You who have come to know Christ no longer belong to that father—your Father is God himself—and you are to speak like Him!"

So Put Off falsehood . . . and speak the truth.

Self-Control, Not Anger

Paul goes on. As you add accessories, here's a second one: self-control. Put Off anger . . . and Put On self-control. "'In your anger do not sin': Do not let the sun go down while you are still angry, and do not give the devil a foothold" (Ephesians 4:26, 27).

Now remember: Paul is drawing a comparison. On the one hand, he describes a typical unbeliever; on the other, a committed Christ-follower. Now these two characters live in the same world. They sit through the same traffic jams, listen to the same tirades from their bosses, endure the same unfair attacks from friends, and absorb the same angry retorts from their kids.

But the unbeliever, if she is true to form, is going to sin when she gets angry about that stuff.

While the believer, *if* she is true to form, will positively reflect the "new self" God is making her to be.

Oh, she'll still get angry; she's just not going to sin in that anger.

Please note this distinction. Paul is not prohibiting anger. In fact, in the original language he's actually saying, "Be angry! Go ahead! Experience the emotion! God created you to feel all that stuff! However—" (you knew there'd be a *however*, didn't you?), "in your anger do not sin."

Paul says that being angry isn't the problem. It's what we do when we're angry. That's the problem.

And an unbeliever will, typically, sin all over the place when she gets angry. How? Well, Paul says, the typical unbeliever stores up anger. She allows Satan to set up camp in that angry spirit and build on it and magnify it and blow the whole deal way out of proportion.

Maybe she explodes in a rage.

Or . . . maybe turns it inward and beats herself up in shame.

Or . . . maybe she'll hold a grudge and pout.

There are all kinds of ways to sin in our anger. And Paul says that the typical unbeliever really knows how to go there.

Then again, so does the Christ-follower. But according to Paul, he's supposed to wear a different garment. Oh, he'll still get angry, even royally ticked off! But here's what the Christian is *not* going to do. He's not going to deny it, discount it, or drive it underground. Neither is he going to store it up and nurse it and curse it and rehearse it over and over until Satan finally takes a match to that parched pile of timber—and *kerblooey!* Bodies fly everywhere. Words are spoken that will never be forgotten. Relationships are destroyed when they could have been restored.

No, because he's a believer—because she's a Christ-follower—they're going to express their anger constructively.

Which means she's going to express it soon so it doesn't grow any larger than it already is. Before the sun goes down, Paul says.

And he's going to take his anger to the right person—and never rage to uninvolved parties. In fact, nobody else will even know there's a problem until the involved party knows first. That's straight from Jesus, folks. That's Matthew 18.

And she's also going to express her anger in a constructive spirit rather than just blowing somebody up. We'll see that again in a moment. She will do it that way because she wants to build up the relationship, not just satisfy her rage by tearing somebody down. She wants to reconcile; she wants healing and restoration to occur.

Now that's quite a makeover, isn't it? And when a believer handles his or her anger in this way, it's a beautiful thing to behold.

A woman came to see me. She was shaking as she said, "I am very angry, but I want to handle this in the right way."

I said, "I commend you for that. Tell me about your anger."

She said, "Someone has let me down, and I'm so angry I'm tempted to just rage and do all kinds of sinful stuff. But I've been praying about it, and I really want to handle this right and honor God with my behavior."

I said, "I'm proud of you. So how can I help? Who are you mad at?"

"You."

Whoa!

That really ticked me off, but I said, "Well, tell me how I made you angry."

She explained the situation; then I explained where I was coming from and why I did what I did. And by the time we talked it through, we met in the middle. I asked for forgiveness and she did the same.

As she walked away, I thought, *Now that's one impressive woman—a believer who walks what she talks. She could have done a lot of sin with that anger. But she didn't. She handled it soon. She handled it with me. And she handled it with grace.*

Do you make that kind of fashion statement when you get angry?

Meaningful Work, Not Stealing

A third accessory is meaningful work. Put Off stealing . . . and Put On meaningful work. "He who has been stealing must steal no longer, but must work, doing something useful with his own hands, that he may have something to share with those in need" (Ephesians 4:28).

Imagine our unbeliever and our Christ-follower as models moving down a runway. Every day they're exposed to the same trinkets and toys. They both see the glitter and sparkle; they both sit in front of their TVs watching the same ads and allurements.

The difference is that the unbeliever—if he's true to form—is going to steal stuff. He's going to steal his employer's time or even product. He's going to cheat on his taxes and lie about his kid's age at the movies. He's going to be involved in doing his best to get something for nothing!

Meanwhile, the believer, *if* she is true to form, is learning the joy of working. She's practicing the discipline of living within her budgetary limits. She's also finding much more pleasure in giving than she ever did in getting. Whether it's giving to people in need or giving to the work of God, she finds great satisfaction in investing in someone and something other than herself.

Now these contrasts have nothing to do with one person being better than the other. It's a nature thing. The Gentile—

the unbeliever—because of his nature, is futile in his thinking and darkened in his understanding. So when those trinkets are dangled in front of him, as they glitter and sparkle and shine, the unbeliever thinks, *That new toy will complete me!* And because he has no other nature but his own, he can't help himself!

But the believer *does* have a different nature—a new self, a new attitude of the mind (see Ephesians 4:23, 24). And so, work is seen as a blessing. And meeting the needs of others becomes such a priority that instead of feeding her greed, she gives to others as they have need.

Helpful Words, Not Put-Downs

A fourth accessory is wholesome speech. Put Off unwholesome talk . . . and Put On words that build up. "Do not let any unwholesome talk come out of your mouths, but only what is helpful for building others up according to their needs, that it may benefit those who listen" (v. 29).

Imagine again our unbeliever and Christ-follower as models moving down the runway of life. If the unbeliever is true to form, his speech will be rotten and putrid. Whether it's profanity or vulgarity or thoughtless verbal put-downs, the Gentile lifestyle is all over that stuff.

But the believer, *if* she is true to form, is going to have a speech pattern marked by words that glorify God and encourage people.

But don't give her any brownie points, because this is a nature thing. Jesus, in Matthew 12, says it's "out of the overflow of the heart [that] the mouth speaks. The good man brings good things out of the good stored up in him, and the evil man brings evil things out of the evil stored up in him" (vv. 34, 35).

And in Ephesians 4, Paul says the good man is good only because he's been made "new." See verse 23? Having been made new, the believer is now expected to *sound* new.

Maybe I'm ultrasensitive about this, but my entire family of origin battles with weight. So whenever I hear someone poke fun at somebody who's chubby, or laugh at someone grossly obese, or grab somebody's belly and kid about "too many Twinkies," I grimace. I don't laugh because I don't think it's funny.

Does that make me better than you? No. It's just that I've experienced, up close and personal, the incredible pain of obesity. And I'm not going to laugh at somebody else's pain.

I had lunch with an attorney friend. His voice was quivering when he said, "Steve, I die every time I hear a lawyer joke. See, I'm doing what God called me to do. I do it well. I do it with integrity. And it breaks my heart when people laugh at my calling."

I'll be honest: part of me wanted to say, "Lighten up, Randy! Plenty of jokes are told about preachers, too!"

Instead I decided that as long as I'm his pastor, I will never again tell a lawyer joke. And that's a real sacrifice because I've got a thick file of them! But I didn't go there because I love Randy, and to talk in a manner that would hurt him would be "unwholesome"!

Let's go deeper. The unbeliever can curse God and it's almost expected. He can put down, trash-talk, and damn anybody and everybody. But the follower of Christ? Hey, if you've had a saving encounter with Jesus, you can't do that!

When I became a Christian at age nine, I thought I was the worst sinner on the planet. But I felt an explosion of divine love and acceptance absolutely washing over my heart, and I've never been the same since. So why in the world would I ever curse the God who saved me? And I don't say that because I'm pristine pure and have never, ever been tempted, much less fallen. I'm saying it because my heart is so thankful to God for His grace, why would I ever want to curse Him?

Then, when I read in Scripture that people are God's treasure, that people are what Christ died for, that the stuff we treasure is going to rust and burn up but people are eternal—that people, above everything else, matter most to God—that makes it really hard for me to curse my fellow man as well.

Not because I'm better, but because I have a new nature.

You do, too, if you're a Christian, and *if* you're living true to that new form, you're going to want to say words that lift people up and inspire and affirm them.

That's the kind of talk that comes from a believer who wants to sound "like God."

Forgiveness, Not Bitterness

The final accessory, forgiveness, is equally tough. Put Off bitterness . . . Put On forgiveness. "Get rid of all bitterness, rage and anger, brawling and slander, along with every form of malice. Be kind and compassionate to one another, forgiving each other, just as in Christ God forgave you" (Ephesians 4:31, 32).

You've got the drill down? The unbeliever, if true to form, holds a grudge. When he's been wronged, he doesn't forget. Instead, he's filled with all kinds of malice and revenge. Like in the movie *The Waterboy,* the unbeliever actually draws on his negative experiences just so he can mow people down and get what he wants.

A new assistant coach had been hired to recruit for the Auburn football team. The head coach was instructing him on the type of player the team wanted: "Do you know the kind of man who gets knocked down and stays down?"

"Yeah, coach, and that's not the kind of man we want for this football team."

The coach said, "Do you know the kind of man that gets knocked down and then he gets up and then he gets knocked down and then he gets up and then he gets knocked down again and stays down?"

The recruiter answered, "Yeah, and that's not the kind of man we want for the Auburn football team."

The coach said, "But there's a certain kind of man who gets knocked down, and he gets up—and he gets knocked down and he gets up—knocked down and gets up—knocked down and gets up—no matter how many times you knock him down, he gets up."

The recruiter answered, "Coach, now *that's* the man we want for the Auburn football team!"

The coach said, "No, that's *not* who we want. We want the dude that's knocking all those dudes down!"

Well, that may be who you want to play football with, and that may be the way Gentiles find empowerment and motivation to stay in the game, but friend, that's not what God looks like.

It's true: bitterness is the most natural response in the world—that's why Gentiles are so good at it. But I agree with Dan Hamilton, who wrote in *Forgiveness,* "Suppressed resentment will never die; it will be held in reserve and nurtured like malignant toadstools in the cellar. Resentment suppressed will never lose its power; like a spark in a gasoline tank, a bit of momentary friction will set off a devastating explosion." [1]

It's true! You feel hurt every time you remember what he did to you. Your memory is like TiVo, just playing and replaying that same old scene, and with each new showing there's a whole new wave of anger.

But if you've got God's Spirit living in you, and if He's busily at work building His strength to sustain you, then instead of bitterness and wrath, instead of finding ways to get even and strike back, you'll want to do your best to look like God. You'll find ways to be kind and gentle and muster the strength you need to freely and fully forgive.

Why? Because that's what God did for you.

GETTING STARTED

That's quite a list, isn't it? And you're probably wondering where to start. I mean, I really do want to make a fashion statement for God. And I'm beginning to realize, I've got a real fashion emergency goin' on! I've got some items in my wardrobe that don't reflect the Christ I claim to follow. So what do I do to get a different wardrobe?

Well, I've heard fashion experts say that the first step in changing your fashion statement is finding the right clothing. The foundation of any wardrobe is the main outfit you've decided to wear. Only then do you start worrying about accessories.

So think for a moment: what do you think would be the first step in correcting your flawed look?

Do you know what Paul says is the first step? Do you know what Paul says is the foundation of a spiritual fashion statement? It's your mind!

I like that. In fashion, when you're trying to create a new look, you spend a lot of time thinking about skin color and hair color, whether you're petite or tall, whether you have a slim frame or there's more of you to love—all of these factors come into play when you're trying to come up with your new look.

And yet the most important factor in your makeover is what you think about yourself right between the ears. It's true! If you think you're unattractive, you'll carry yourself like you're unattractive. If you think your teeth are crooked, you'll smile like your teeth are crooked! If you think your shape isn't shapely enough? You'll accessorize with overcoats.

Your mind plays a vitally significant role in what you become. It really does.

And the same is true in the spiritual realm. We've been talking about accessories, what you add to the outfit you've already selected. But the foundation is your mind. The kind of person you've decided you want to be. The kind of statement you want your life to make.

It all begins in the mind.

In Ephesians 4:17 Paul says that the Gentile lives the way he lives because he's become futile in his thinking. Darkened in his mind, he's excluded God from his life and that decision has led to hard-heartedness and a callousness that eventually causes an unbeliever to just give himself over to sensuality and greed and an addictive lifestyle that lusts for more and more.

And it's that kind of mind that leads to lying and raging and stealing and cursing and slandering and abusing people.

And friend, the only way you can avert your spiritual fashion emergency is to change the condition of your mind. Paul says that you've got to be "made new in the attitude of your minds" (v. 23). And when that renewal, that extreme makeover, that amazing transformation takes place, you start living in the likeness of God—you start doing things the way He would.

By that I mean you start telling the truth. You handle anger constructively. You work hard and budget well so you can give generously. You use your mouth to empower people, not destroy people. You're tender and forgiving, even when you've been wronged.

To make the change, begin first in the mind. So . . . how's your mind?

In chapter three, we're going to talk about that very issue. We're going to talk about how you can reprogram your brain by filling your mind with God's mind.

If you really want to make a change, keep reading.

CHAPTER 3

THE *X* FACTOR

THE LONGER I LIVE the more I'm convinced—no matter who you are or where you live, no matter your profession or financial condition—there's something about you that you wish you could change.

I realize where you'll try to run with that, but the "something" I have in mind runs much deeper than the amount of hair you wish you still had on your head or the contour of your misshapen nose or even the breadth of your hyperextended belly. Trust me, we *all* wish we could do a makeover that would transform those external flaws.

But the changes I have in mind have to do with those not-so-obvious *internal* alterations. You know, the part of you that would like to be more confident in social settings or more relaxed when you give your monthly sales report? Face it. Some of us wish we were more outgoing or less anxious or not so—dare I say it?—*borrr*ing. Others wish we weren't held hostage by some nasty habit or that snarly attitude we battle. Still others wish we could put the brakes on our raging temper or a bridle on our vicious, out-of-control tongue.

That's the kind of change I'm talking about. So let's take a poll. Don't you have at least one internal dysfunction that really bugs you, yet—no matter how you try—you just can't seem to overcome it?

That's what I thought! And though you've bought a mountain of self-help tapes, read Tony Robbins, and watched endless reruns of Dr. Phil—you can't make a dent in that monster, can you?

Well, that's where Trading Places comes into play. I mean, let's face it: we all would like to make a change. But then, when we come across a list like the one in chapter two and realize that some of the essential accessories of a Christ-led life include such things as honesty in your personal and business transactions, expressing anger in healthy ways, commitment to hard work, a generous spirit, and using words to encourage people, not trash them—and on top of all that a heart that freely forgives—when you look at a list like that and then you look at your life, you can't help wonder, *How will I ever get there?*

Or maybe you look at a list such as the one in Galatians 5, a list of nine positive character traits that none of us has even come close to mastering: "love, joy, peace, patience, kindness, goodness, faithfulness, gentleness" and even "self-control" (vv. 22, 23). If you're like me, you look at that list and think, *I've got SOME of those down SOME of the time.* But "some . . . sometimes" isn't good enough . . . is it?

And that's why Trading Places is so vital. Because Trading Places, as we're using it here, is the only God-guaranteed method for finding true, lasting change.

Because even if you did bump into Tony Robbins in some elevator somewhere—you know, like Shallow Hal? Even that won't help you make a lasting change. Because the only power that can truly change your life is the same power that caused Jesus to walk out of that tomb.

And that power is freely available to you in the form of the Holy Spirit of God at work in your life. And it's that power that can transform your most glaring internal weaknesses into positive, awe-inspiring tributes to the God who made and loves you.

THE POWER OF GOD

This power is so all-encompassing that God can take your most unchangeable reality—namely, your past (talk about cast in concrete)—and can, the Bible says, cancel your past! He can take the ugly history of your life and absolutely blast it into oblivion!

He can take your problems, too. You know, those problems that eat away at your insides? That keep you up nights watching reruns and surfing the Web? Those problems are like the Adidas commercial: Impossible is nothing! It really is. If . . . *if* the Holy Spirit of God is at work within you.

In fact, God's power is so great that His Holy Spirit can even change your personality! Those obnoxious parts inside you that drive other people bonkers? He can change even those.

Now, not the kind of surgi-center, in one day and out the next with a cute buggy nose instead of a ski slope kind of make-over. No, the kind of change the Holy Spirit brings could take a whole lifetime to get right, but here's the good news: it always unfolds according to a simple, two-phase process.

The Two Gears of Change

The cool thing about this miracle makeover is that here are no toll-free phone numbers to dial, no tapes to buy, and no "call before midnight tonight" deals to strike.

Phase one. The only thing you've got to do to actualize God's incredible changing power is . . . anybody remember? You've got to wait. You've got to "wait for the LORD." We've been calling that response the Great Exchange, because when you decide to "wait"—in that moment of pause when instead of charging ahead in your own strength, you wait for, you expect, you look for, you put your hope in God—in that moment, He will exchange your weakness for His strength!

And as Isaiah so eloquently put it, that's when you're strong enough to mount up with wings like an eagle. To run without getting tired. To walk and walk and walk without ever becoming weary.

Let's call this phase one in God's strategic plan for making a change. And we'll call it phase one because the Great Exchange begins, essentially, in your moment of salvation—that moment of faith when you decide to put your hope in God and God alone. Other Great Exchanges will follow, as I mentioned in chapter one, because this "exchange" is a lifelong process. But it all gets started in that first burst of faith. That's when, the Bible says, God immediately changes you!

Second Corinthians 5:17 says, "If anyone is in Christ, he is a new creation; the old has gone, the new has come!" In other words, in the moment you commit your life to Jesus Christ, you experience an instantaneous transformation! You're not the same person anymore. Instead, you are a brand-spanking, drive-out-of-the-showroom, absolutely N-E-W *new* creature!

And that's why salvation is often called being born again. It doesn't mean you get reincarnated; it means you get a do-over! Much more than just turning over a new leaf, you receive a new life—as God gives you the incredible opportunity to start your life all over again.

Phase two. Now track with me: by calling salvation phase one, it would appear that I'm implying that there must also be a phase two. Guess what? There is!

And phase two is called sanctification. Now I realize . . . *sanctification* is a pretty scary word—but don't bug out on me, because it has a really simple meaning: sanctification is God's process for changing you.

That's it?

That's it. That's essentially what the word means. And here's the primary difference between the two phases: salvation is an event— a once-in-a-lifetime moment—but sanctification is a process. An ongoing process for helping you close the gap between how God views you, positionally, in Christ and how you actually live, practically, in your daily life. It's God's word for what's happening inside you as you conform your life more and more into the image of Jesus.

And although salvation happens in an instant, sanctification is our constant companion till the day we die. And while salvation is a work that is fully accomplished by God and God alone, sanctification requires an investment from me. The change that happens is still GOD'S deal, not mine—but I do have a response to make, an essential response.

Do you remember how we described it? We called it Putting Off and Putting On. Right? And folks, that's my part in this process of change.

A Divine Partnership for Change

See, if God's great makeover in your life is ever to come to be, there has to be a partnership. God doesn't just zap people, and all of sudden you're joyful and loving and gentle and thoughtful and gracious and forgiving! NO! It's a partnership. God has a part to play, but so do you.

I've already told you that God is good for His part of the deal. God will supply, but (hang with me) we must apply. God has given His Holy Spirit, but we still have to exert some "holy sweat." He's given us the vine of His abiding strength, but we've got to stay connected to that vine. He's developed a makeover plan absolutely guaranteed to give you a great new look, but there's some Putting Off and Putting On that only you can do.

And therein lies the problem. We read Ephesians 4, and we decide it's time to Put Off some stuff, right? And to Put On some other stuff instead?

And we're serious about it! I mean, no holds barred, baby! I am making a change! Yet, a couple of days later (or in some cases, maybe only hours), we're back in the closet putting that ratty old stuff right back on again . . . right?

Are there any honest souls here willing to admit that's exactly what's happened to you?

Because that's the way life works! I mean, I really want to make this change, but . . . I like my life as it is, too!

I heard about an Arizona town that had been totally flooded, so the state flew in six helicopters to rescue the stranded towns-people. By their calculations, they had already flown out the entire population, but there still were a whole lot of people down there! So they kept retrieving folks, until they figured again and realized that they'd brought out thirty-five percent more people than actually lived there!

They sent in a team to find out what was going on. You know what they discovered? The townspeople loved the helicopter ride so much, they were boating back in so they could get another ride!

Isn't that a hoot? And how real! Are you kidding me? Yeah, I want rescued, but I like helicopter rides, too. I know I'm playing with fire by being in this relationship, but it's kind of exciting, you know? No, I don't want to die, but using this stuff . . . well, I'm having the time of my life right now!

And so you Put Off—but then turn around and put the same thing right back on, but then off again, on again, off again, on again. To the point that change is more discussed than it is displayed!

But it doesn't have to be that way. In fact, the Bible clearly declares that lasting change really is possible! That book is jampacked with stories and illustrations all designed to help you see that the "new you" you want to be is not a pipe dream—it can happen! You really can change!

But you need more than just personal motivation to change; you need to make the Great Exchange. You need to find your strength in God.

And while it *is* important that you respond to God's power with a strong commitment to Putting Off ugly behaviors that rob you of God's best for you—you need more than just a minor adjustment here and there. You need a complete overhaul. Dinking around on the fringe of your life is what keeps you racing back to those old destructive behaviors.

You need—are you ready for this?—you need a *new mind.* A new way of thinking. A different set of perspectives for what is important in life. And that new mind is God's *X* Factor for changes in you that will last.

Are you following the progression of God's formula?

You need to put your hope in God . . . by "waiting for" God.

And you need to make lifestyle changes based on what you know God wants to see in you.

However, if those changes are to stand the test of time, you've got to change the way you think—or the change you make today will be lost come tomorrow.

Paul put it this way: "So I tell you this, and insist on it in the Lord, that you must no longer live as the Gentiles do, in the futility of their thinking" (Ephesians 4:17). And instead, you need "to be made new in the attitude of your minds" (v. 23).

HOW TO MAKE YOUR OLD MIND NEW

I find it intriguing that Paul strikes exactly the same theme in Romans 12 that he addressed with the Ephesians we saw in chapter 2. But instead of saying, "Don't live like the Gentiles" (see Ephesians 4:17), he says, in Romans, "Do not conform any longer to the pattern of this world" (12:2). But check it out . . . it's just a different way of saying the exact same thing.

Now I have always enjoyed the Phillips paraphrase of that verse. Phillips puts it, "Don't let the world around you squeeze you into its own mold." You know what I think of every time I read that? Jell-O!

I mean, who can't relate to Jell-O? Last year, 400 million boxes of Jell-O were purchased. And why not? It's not every food you can play with . . . or wrestle in.

And the amazing thing about Jell-O is that it can take on so many personalities. Put it in a bowl, it's shaped like a bowl. Pour it in a glass, it becomes like a glass. Chunk all kinds of fruit and nuts in it—and it congeals around that stuff, creating all sorts of surreal, impressionistic images. And thanks to the Jell-O Jigglers recipe, you can even make Jell-O cutouts and eat them with your hands!

Now Jell-O is basically the glutinous material from animal bone, skin, and connective tissue combined with food coloring and flavored sugar. It's fat-free, cholesterol-free, and only eighty calories per half cup.

Why do I bring up such an apparently unrelated and seemingly bizarre topic? Because technicians at St. Jerome Hospital in Batavia, New York, hooked up an EEG machine to a mound of lime Jell-O. You know what they found?

Jell-O has qualities virtually identical to the human brain.[1] Ain't that a kick? Hey, it's not that surprising to me because Jell-O is what we do . . . isn't it? Stick me in any given situation, and I will tend to conform to whatever expectations I find there.

But put me over here in this particular circumstance? And I'll play that role, too, because I'm Jell-O! And so are you.

But Paul says, "Don't let that happen to you! Don't be like Jell-O! Don't conform to the mold!"

Except that it's written in the present tense, so it actually means, "*Keep on* not being conformed." It's a constant process, OK? A continual effort not to conform to—to refuse to congeal your life around—"the pattern of this world."

The Pattern of This World

Exactly what *is* this world's pattern? It's basically the same kind of stuff we saw in Ephesians. The Gentile lifestyle is, essentially, the pattern of our world.

And you know it's true! Because our world is all about lying to get out of a jam. Stealing so you can get something for nothing. Raging out control so people will do what you want them to do. Tossing around trash talk and verbal put-downs in order to strut your stuff. And harboring bitterness so those who hurt you never forget that they hurt you. That's the pattern, Paul is saying.

The apostle John adds some insight: "Do not love the world or anything in the world. If anyone loves the world, the love of the Father is not in him. For everything in the world—[*Check out his list!*] the cravings of sinful man, the lust of his eyes and the boasting of what he has and does—comes not from the Father but from the world" (1 John 2:15, 16).

Every day, our minds are bombarded with sights and sounds designed to appeal to our sinful cravings, our lustful appetites, and the prideful boasting of what we have and what we can do.

And these temptations produce within us desires and feelings that make us want to act out those cravings.

And that is the pattern of our world: to see the images that feed our ego, to think about what it would be like to embrace those images—and think enough about it that you actually want to embrace them—until, ultimately, we do embrace them.

But Paul says, "Don't go there!" Don't be conformed to that predicable pattern. Instead, "Be transformed!" It's the same word from which we get *metamorphosis*, which means a total change—inside and out. Paul is saying, "I want you to be totally changed, to live in such a way that what you Put Off stays off and what you Put On stays on."

Now keep reading, because the only way that metamorphosis can happen is if you *renew your mind*.

Something has to change about the way you think. You cannot go on thinking the way the world around you thinks and not eventually give in and be conformed to it. You've got to have—I've got to have—a change of mind.

And that change only comes from a day by day, week by week, year in and year out renewal process.

But having a change of mind is the only way you won't conform to our world—because only then are you able to see through our world's silly, stupid schemes.

The Mind of Christ

The Bible calls this new mind "the mind of Christ" (1 Corinthians 2:16). And the mind of Christ is nothing other than the ability to look at life as Jesus does . . . to see our world as He sees it. To discern what is good and not what just appears to be good. To discern the eternal from what is merely temporal.

The mind of Christ says, "I'm not here just for my own gratification; I'm on this planet to serve God and to advance His cause."

The only way I know to get that mind of Christ is to hold tightly to God's Word.

Hebrews 4:12 says, "The word of God is living and active. Sharper than any double-edged sword, it penetrates even to dividing soul and spirit, joints and marrow; it judges the thoughts and attitudes of the heart."

In other words, God's Word is not dead . . . and it's not dull. It lives! And it cuts!

The fact that it lives means that it's just as vital today as the day God spoke it into existence.

And the fact that it cuts refers to the power of the Bible to expose the garbage of our culture. To cut through the fog. To lay bare the lame excuses we offer, the intricate rationalizations we manufacture, and the ugly blame we hide behind. It cuts to the core of reality and penetrates right to the heart of what is right and what is true.

That's why Paul said to the Ephesians, "Take . . . the sword of the Spirit" (6:17). And use it to slay those evil dragons and cut down those excuses and lies. But he also says, "Take the helmet of salvation." The sword is offensive, the helmet is defensive. If you're ever going to renew that world-saturated mind of yours, you've got to put on the helmet. You've got to place a guard at the fore of your mind as a sentinel that is "useful for teaching, rebuking, correcting and training in righteousness" (2 Timothy 3:16). Then you can know God's will without doubt—and, in fact, "you will be able to test and approve what God's will is—his good, pleasing and perfect will" (Romans 12:2).

See, that's how lasting change happens! Once you've tapped into God's power and begun to make some lifestyle changes, once you've started filling your mind with God's mind—you won't be foggy about what His will happens to be.

The Power of God's Word

The only way I know to renew your mind is to get an absolute death grip on God's Word. The Bible, folks—and the Bible alone—is how God empowers His children to counteract all the lies that swarm around us every day.

That's why, at the church I serve, we are committed to teaching God's Word every single time we gather. And that's why a key component of our small groups is all about grappling with truth and getting a handle on the Word. And it's also why, in our discipleship classes, a key component of that teaching plan is about training people to get into the Word for themselves on an ongoing, daily basis.

And I believe in the power of the Word so strongly, I'm willing to say—without apology or embarrassment—that if you're not currently part of a church where God's Word is faithfully taught, if you are not systematically receiving a spiritual feeding where the main course is absolutely lathered with the transforming truths found in the Bible and the Bible alone . . . then you need to find a church that does teach like that.

Because it is only by a systematic and consistent intake of God's Word that we can overhaul our minds. Then, instead of acting like lumps of Jell-O, we can be transformed into stones like spiritual granite! Strong, firm, and settled in our convictions.

Understand, when you have the mind of Christ at work in your life—oh, you'll still be tempted. But here's what will happen when you are:

When you're tempted to sell out to some drastic change in your appearance, you'll remember that God doesn't look at what man looks at . . . God looks at the heart (see 1 Samuel 16:7).

And when you're tempted to grab power, you'll recall the words of Paul, a man who rose to the very pinnacle of all things Jewish, yet he said, "Whatever was to my profit I now consider loss for the sake of Christ. . . . I consider them rubbish, that I may gain Christ and be found in him" (Philippians 3:7-9).

And when money is all you think about, the mind of Christ will remind you to think about this: "What good will it be for a man if he gains the whole world, yet forfeits his soul?" (Matthew 16:26).

And when you're tempted to think that pleasure is where it's at? You'll remember Proverbs 21:17: "He who loves pleasure will become poor."

I'm sure you know men who have left behind spouse and children—not to mention job and reputation—simply because "I've got to go find myself." But you know what? They never come back and say, "Well, praise the Lord! I found myself in Elmo, Utah . . . can you believe that?!" No, what they say—after it's way too late—is, "I messed up. I never did find myself."

Women, in their middle years, are tempted to say, "All my life I've done for others . . . now it's time to think about me!" Ask 'em after the fact if they're happy. "No . . . not really."

The next time you're tempted to indulge yourself, to pursue pleasure even at the cost of everybody else in your life, remember Solomon's sad takeaway that pleasure is meaningless, "a chasing after the wind" (Ecclesiastes 2:11). I could go on all day like this:

When you're tempted to worry, the Bible says pray.

When you're filled with panic, Jesus promises peace.

When you're prompted toward revenge, God says, "That's *my* deal . . . you turn the other cheek."

When it feels good and you want to do it, Jesus says, "Not my will, but thine be done."

When you're drawn into compromise, when God says no, but every fiber of your being screams yes, the mind of Christ will remind you—there is a way of escape! (See 1 Corinthians 10:13.)

When you say, "I can't do that," the Bible says you can do *all* things through Christ who gives you strength (see Philippians 4:13).

It doesn't say you can do all things through steroids. Or education. Or financial strength, success, or positive thinking. NO! I can do all things . . . through Christ!

I know what you're thinking: *I want to live like that! I do! I want to live like Christ! I want a new mind! But how? Where do I start? Isn't there some map to direct me . . . some kind of mentor . . . some sort of travel guide who can come alongside me and help me find the way? Is there?* Please listen to me: Jesus has already given you everything you need to make your change. *Everything.*

Spirit Power

Before Jesus returned to the Father, He gave us the Holy Spirit, a companion who will always come alongside us and guide us into truth—reinforcing and reestablishing that new mind and all its rightful impulses. And that's why Paul, in Galatians 5:16, issues this unyielding command: "So I say, live by the Spirit, and you will not gratify the desires of the sinful nature."

Please understand, change is a choice. You can't just passively sit around doing nothing and expect to somehow become more loving and more forgiving! You've got to make a conscious decision to "live by the Spirit."

Paul said elsewhere that we must "count [ourselves] dead to sin but alive to God in Christ Jesus" (Romans 6:11). We must refuse to "let sin reign" in our mortal bodies (Romans 6:12). We must never, ever lose heart in doing good (see Galatians 6:9).

You see, only the Spirit can produce the kind of change you want to see happen, but if you refuse to play the role God has assigned to you—if you fail to "live by the Spirit"—then the change God desires for you will never happen.

So how do you live by the Spirit? Galatians 5:25 says you live by the Spirit by keeping in step with the Spirit.

That phrase "keep in step with" is a military term, and it means to keep the pace. To march in a disciplined, orderly fashion. And that's so cool because our sinful nature is constantly seeking alternative paths. In my human nature, I'm drawn in a thousand directions, and every one of them has the capacity to destroy me. But Paul tells us that if we'll just march to the beat of a different drummer, if we'll just tune out every other competing voice and listen only to the Spirit's call—God will fill our lives with everything we need to make a change that lasts!

But here's how it works: to have that renewed mind, you've got to fill your mind with God's mind, and you also need to live "by the Spirit" by "keep[ing] in step with the Spirit."

Some of you may be struggling with what that means, so perhaps some insight from Jesus will help. Jesus' men were also struggling with this, so Jesus said, in effect, "Men, I am the vine; you are the branches. That's how this works. I'm the core, and you flow out from the core." Therefore, Jesus said, "If a man remains in me and I in him, he will bear much fruit; apart from me you can do nothing" (John 15:5).

The word *remains* means "to dwell, to rest . . . to abide," in this case, with Jesus. Sounds like "keep in step," doesn't it?

Listen, that word *remains* is the great need of your life! Because if you really want to change, it's not your job to agonize and fret and beat yourself up about it! It's not your job to grind out fruit. It's not even your job to renew your mind. Your job is this: you've got to keep in step with the Spirit.

Living Connected and Dependent

So the only thing standing between you and the kind of person you've always wanted to be is this: you've got to live a connected, dependent life. You need to willingly exchange your dreams for His design. You need to give Jesus free and complete operating power in your life. You need to put all of your hope and trust in Him.

Stop trusting in some set of rules or some form of outward religiosity, and instead just cling to Christ. Make it your ambition to follow footprint for footprint with His Holy Spirit.

Now please! Don't let your eyes glaze over! Because if there ever was truth, this is truth: if you want to bear fruit, if you want to cultivate a life of love and joy and a forgiving spirit and all these other qualities, if you really want the mind of Christ—and if you really want to make a change—you've got to glue yourself to Jesus. And if you don't? I mean, if you think you've got a better plan? Jesus said it, not me: "You can do nothing" (John 15:5).

Now we don't really believe that. We think we can do it. Even more, we think we *ought* to do it! So we operate under huge loads of guilt. We respond to heavy-handed manipulation as we struggle and strain to be like Christ. Because we want to make fruit! But that's not our job. And when we try? The fruit we do produce is a phony imitation of the real thing.

I mean, think about it: have you ever seen a lemon pump iron? Have you ever seen an apple eat vitamins? Never. All fruit can do is just hang on the vine, and the vine shoots into that little blob of potential all the necessary nutrients that will transform that potential into a plump, juicy, tasty treat.

And that's all you can do, too. All you've got to do to make a change—are you with me?—is just hang on the vine. Just remain in Jesus. If you do that, Jesus promises He'll produce the fruit; He'll give you your makeover!

"What a strange cow," said the man from the city to his farmer cousin. "Why doesn't that cow have any horns?"

"Well," explained the country boy, "some cows are born without horns and never had any, and others shed theirs. Some we de-horn, and some breeds aren't supposed to have horns at all. There are lots of reasons why some cows ain't got horns. But the reason that cow ain't got horns is that it ain't a cow—it's a horse."

A lot of Christians are stretching and straining, striving hard to change their lives—and all they're becoming is tired. They're horses trying to be cows. Well, it may be a cliché, but it's true: the Christian life is not difficult—it's impossible! It has been lived in perfection only by one, Jesus. If it is to be lived successfully by you, it will only happen as you keep in step with Spirit.

Yet how many believers, when they feel the loss of spiritual power, go to a conference? They're not experiencing what they think they need to experience, so they think, *I need to read the Bible more. I need to pray more. I need to go to church more! Then everything will be fine.*

No, it won't! Because that's not how it works. That's not how change happens! If you want to be great in God's kingdom, you've got to get a new mind. You've got to keep in step with the Spirit! You've got to cling to Jesus' vine! Don't go on a pilgrimage to the Holy Land or do something religious like get baptized in water shipped in from the Jordan River. Don't start wearing religious trinkets; don't read a religious book; don't buy another sermon tape.

If you want to make a change—get close to Jesus! Stop doing all that crazy jazz and start walking footprint for footprint with the Lord.

PART TWO

SO FAR WE'VE LEARNED that lasting change has three major components:

I exchange my weakness for God's strength by refusing to charge ahead and by choosing to wait on Him—the Great Exchange.

I use my newfound strength to develop character qualities that help me live in the likeness of God—Putting Off and Putting On.

I keep in step with the Spirit, and I glue myself to Jesus—the *X* Factor.

In part two, we're going to watch as these three components are fleshed out in the lives of some of God's most famous followers. Chances are good you'll see some of yourself in each of their stories.

CHAPTER 4

TRADING LONELINESS FOR LOYALTY

SOMEHOW, *LONELY* DOESN'T EVEN BEGIN to describe her. Living in a foreign land, adapting to a strange culture, too soon widowed—and now, both of her sons are also dead?

Not exactly how Naomi planned things would go. She and Elimelech just wanted to escape Israel during the famine. Maybe their boys would get married and maybe even make some grand-kids . . . But then, after the famine, together, as a family, they'd wave good-bye to the land of Moab, go home to Bethlehem, and live happily ever after.

We don't really know what dreams this couple had, but you've got to know they had some. All we know for sure is: "In the days when the judges ruled, there was a famine in the land, and a man from Bethlehem in Judah, together with his wife and two sons, went to live for a while in the country of Moab" (Ruth 1:1).

Unfortunately, "for a while" lasted ten years! And instead of growing her family, Naomi no longer even had a family. Her hus-band, her sons—everybody she knew and loved . . . was gone.

Well, not *every*body. Naomi's sons had, in fact, gotten mar-ried. "They married Moabite women, one named Orpah [*no, not*

Oprah!] and the other Ruth. After they had lived there about ten years, both Mahlon and Kilion also died, and Naomi was left without her two sons and her husband" (vv. 4, 5).

So Ruth and Orpah were still around, but if you've ever talked with someone recently widowed, you know they were no comfort. They had their own grief to endure—waking up in the middle of the night, wishing he was there . . . turning to ask a question, only to remember, *We'll never talk again* . . . straining to hear the latch at the door and that familiar "Honey, I'm home!"

So much for hanging out in Moab "for a while." So much for waiting out the storm and then back to Bethlehem with her multiplying tribe in tow.

DISAPPOINTED BY GOD

Have you ever been there? Have you ever been disappointed by God? I mean, we just assume that our Pleasantville existence— our idyllic, Stepford-like wonderworld—will just keep rolling along! We even tend to believe it's God's job to make sure the party never ends!

It's my job to pray, pay the bills, go to church, be nice to the wife and kids—and not beat the dog; it's God's job to keep the blessings flowing.

Nice dream . . . but it seldom happens that way. It didn't happen to Naomi that way. *At least Ruth and Orpah still live near home!* Naomi must have thought. *Besides, they're young! They can remarry and still have babies! Not me.*

But hang on! Sure they're young, but they married someone of another race, invariably angering their own people! So it's not like their dance cards are gonna fill up, either.

Search for a Family

There you have it: three widows in search of a family. Together . . . yet very much alone. Had Elvis asked them his question, there's no doubt how that sad trio would have replied—"Yeah, I *am* lonesome tonight. And tomorrow night, too."

And that's why Naomi, most lonesome of all, stridently announced, "I'm going home! I need to be around people who know me and share heritage. I love you, Ruth . . . you, too, Orpah . . . but I've got to go home!"

Have you ever "had it up to here" with something? Have you ever been so disgusted with your job, or your mate, or the kids, that you just couldn't take it anymore?

It's not so much the fatigue that does it—although life can be exhausting. And it's not so much the routine that drags you down, either. Most often, it's the sense of unfairness that nails you. "I mean, God, why'd you let us come to Moab, if my family was just gonna die anyway? If we had stayed in Bethlehem, I'd have died, too. But instead, I'm here alone in this God-forsaken land. Hey, there are Ruth and Orpah. But they don't have a life, either! I've got to go . . . I've just *got* to go!"

So Naomi "set out on the road that would take them back to the land of Judah. Then Naomi said to her two daughters-in-law, 'Go back . . . to your mother's home. May the LORD show kindness to you, as you have shown to your dead and to me. May the LORD grant that each of you will find rest in the home of another husband.' Then she kissed them" (vv. 7-9).

I include verse 9 because I don't want you to think Naomi was trying to ditch dead wood! She loved those girls and wanted them to be happy, even if she never would be! She wanted them to get married again and have babies—something that was certainly not in her future!

So she said, "Return home, my daughters. . . ." *You go find a new life!* "It is more bitter for me than for you, because the LORD's hand has gone out against me!" (vv. 12, 13).

So after another round of hugging and crying (this is a female trio, after all), Orpah agrees and heads home. Ruth, however, doesn't agree. From the human perspective, she should have. I can hear her thinking, *If I have any chance at all at a new life, I should stay here among my own kind! Naomi's great, but if I live with an old maid, I could die an old maid! And as much as I love her—she's not gonna be for me what I need!*

Talk about a defining moment! Would she charge ahead and make her own way, or would she choose to wait for God? Ruth could easily have made a case for change based on a very self-driven premise: *If I'm ever gonna stop being lonely, I need to put off old Naomi and put on a new Ruth! An unattached, attractive, and yes, gentlemen, available Ruth—makin' life boogie to the rhythm of a brand new babe—named Ruth!* (Sorry.)

A Loyal Friend

And who would have blamed her? Instead, something inside told her that loyalty would have a pay-off. So she said those now-famous words, words set to music and considered among the most selfless words ever spoken:

"Don't urge me to leave you or to turn back from you. Where you go I will go, and where you stay I will stay. Your people will be my people and your God my God. Where you die I will die, and there I will be buried. May the LORD deal with me, be it ever so severely, if anything but death separates you and me" (vv. 16, 17).

Wow! Do you have a friend like that? A friend who knows your every flaw, yet refuses to walk away or write you off—no matter what?

Someone said you can tell a real friend when you call him from jail. If he asks, "Where?" he's your friend. If he asks, "Why?" he's not.

Do you have a friend like that?

You may think, *I don't need anybody!*

Oh, really? Even Superman needed Lois Lane. And Spider-man? He needed MJ. Batman had Robin. Charlie had his angels. Andy had Barney. And until recently, Shaq had Kobe.

Who do you have?

If the answer is "nobody," no wonder you're struggling. You have no one to help you gain perspective. No one to help you look at your circumstances with objectivity. No one to help infuse you with courage or hug you when you need a hug. To stand beside you when "alone" is more than you can bear.

If you don't have someone like that, I challenge you—find that someone. God says, "It is not good . . . to be alone" (Genesis 2:18). King Solomon said, "Two are better than one" (Ecclesiastes 4:9). And you know what? They're both right.

Two Are Better

And that's why Ruth clung to her mother-in-law. Even though, in her mind, it meant she'd never bear children, she stayed true to her friend.

"So the two women went on until they came to Bethlehem. When they arrived in Bethlehem, the whole town was stirred because of them, and the women exclaimed, 'Can this be Naomi?'

"'Don't call me Naomi,' she told them. 'Call me Mara, because the Almighty has made my life very bitter. I went away full, but the LORD has brought me back empty. . . . The LORD has afflicted me; the Almighty has brought misfortune upon me'" (Ruth 1:19-21).

I told you she'd had it. She was hurting, and in the safe environs of "finally home," she let it all out. All the venom, the bitterness, and the heartache of God's "unfairness"—all of it just spewed from her lips.

And the amazing thing is, Ruth didn't try to correct her. She knew Naomi's heart because Naomi was the reason Ruth had come to believe in God in the first place. Ruth knew that this season of grief would pass.

Besides, she had more on her plate than Naomi's bad attitude. Actually, she *didn't* have anything on her plate—and that was the problem! They needed to eat! And if they were ever going to eat, Ruth had to do something!

Have you ever been there? You're in a hole—with no money, no power, and no resources to care for yourself—and all you can do is just trust God and take it one day at a time. I know it's hard to believe, but that's actually a very positive place to be. Because when you can't help yourself, you get *real* receptive to God's help.

Ruth could do very little to change her circumstance, but the one thing she could do was find food. So she said, "Let me go to the fields and pick up the leftover grain behind anyone in whose eyes I find favor" (2:2). There's so much she couldn't do, but what she could do was Put Off her fear and Put On some hard work.

And that's exactly what she did.

What Ruth didn't know—how could she have known?—is that the field she chose to pick belonged to a wealthy, middle-aged man named Boaz. Scripture says it well, "As it turned out, she found herself working in a field belonging to Boaz, who was [*get this!*] from the clan of Elimelech" (v. 3).

Elimelech? Where have we heard that name before?

That's right, Elimelech was Ruth's deceased father-in-law! Boaz noticed Ruth's hard work and graciously offered her a safe haven on his property—protecting her from the assaults that awaited most women of meager means. He warned his men not to touch her (see v. 9). Even more, he provided her all the food and water she'd require—and even a place to rest when she got tired.

You can imagine how stunned Ruth was by all this attention! When she expressed her gratitude, Boaz said, "I've been told all about what you have done for your mother-in-law since the death of your husband—how you left your father and mother and your homeland and came to live with a people you did not know before. May the LORD repay you for what you have done. May you be richly rewarded by the LORD, the God of Israel, under whose wings you have come to take refuge" (vv. 11, 12).

Kinsman-Redeemer

According to Jewish law, when a woman's husband died, the closest male relative had the right and obligation to marry her and assume her late husband's name and property. Boaz knew that he was not Ruth's closest male relative, but what he didn't know was that he was about to become Ruth's "kinsman-redeemer" anyway.

Ruth had no clue that Boaz was family—but Naomi knew. So returning loyalty for loyalty, she told Ruth what she should do.

I hope you can see God at work in this story. Because the truth is, His fingerprints are all over the place. Ruth could have never arranged that moment.

I mention that because I want you to see that what may seem to you to be a senseless or even hopeless situation is, in the hands of God, the working out of His perfect purpose for your life. You can't see the whole picture, so it doesn't make sense. Like Naomi, you think God's out to get you. That He's mad at you. That He's trying, piece by piece, to destroy you.

Meanwhile, Ruth is picking grain in a foreigner's field. To her, it's just another attempt to get through another day. There's no thought, even for tomorrow. This is just about surviving today. Yet Naomi tells her about Jewish law and what she should do about it.

In obedience, Ruth does as she's told. She lies down at Boaz's feet—and asks him to spread his cloak over her, in a pledge of protection for her life.

He responds, saying, "My daughter, don't be afraid. I will do for you all you ask" (3:11). Then he explains the problem. He said, "Although it is true that I am near of kin, there is a kinsman-redeemer nearer than I. . . . If he wants to redeem, good; let him redeem. But if he is not willing, . . . I will do it (vv. 12:13)."

Ruth was understandably upset. She loved Boaz and didn't even know that other relative! But Naomi said, "Wait, my daughter." (There's that word again.) "Stick it in neutral, girl," Naomi was saying. "You couldn't have manufactured it to this point anyway—so let's just let things play out. I have a sneaking suspicion that 'the man will not rest until the matter is settled today'" (v. 18).

Sure enough, Boaz quickly finalized the legal arrangements—and before the ink was dry on the contract, "Boaz took Ruth and she became his wife. Then he went to her, and the LORD enabled her to conceive, and she gave birth to a son" (4:13).

When the women of the city heard the news—the same women who had earlier heard Naomi whine—they said to Naomi, "'Praise be to the LORD, who this day has not left you without a kinsman-redeemer. May [your grandson] become famous throughout Israel! He will renew your life and sustain you in your old age. For your daughter-in-law, who loves you and who is better to you than seven sons, has given him birth.'

"Then Naomi took the child, laid him in her lap and cared for him. The women living there said, 'Naomi has a son.' And they named him Obed" (vv. 14-17).

FOUR PASSAGES NOT TO MISS

And that's the story of Ruth and Naomi. It's a great story. But if you think that's something, hang on—because I'm going to tell you the story behind the story. I'm going to show you four passages that, if you blast through the book of Ruth too quickly, you might miss. But I don't want you to miss this.

The Beginning of Harvest

"So Naomi returned from Moab accompanied by Ruth the Moabitess, her daughter-in-law, arriving in Bethlehem as the barley harvest was beginning" (1:22).

Remember the context: Naomi has returned to Bethlehem. Her husband is dead. Her sons are dead. She's not only miserable and depressed—she's bitter, desperate, and up-to-here with God. But she came back—do you see it?—"as the barley harvest was beginning." In other words, it was party time in Bethlehem! Have you ever been at a party when you didn't feel like partyin'?

Folks, there'd been a famine in the land for ten years. Finally, the famine is over. It's harvest time—and all the townies who had lived through that mess? They're having a ball!

That's the scene: Everybody is happy—except Naomi.

Her old friends recognize her—they're thrilled to see her! Until she opened her mouth. "Don't call me Naomi. *Naomi* means 'pleasant one.' But you will find, my dear pretties, that Moab changed me. I'm not 'pleasant' anymore. So call me Mara, because I'm a bitter, old woman. I left with a full life, I return empty. I left with a husband and two sons, I return alone. I've got nothing left."

Then she said, "The LORD has afflicted me; the Almighty has brought misfortune upon me" (v. 21). But don't give her any grief; you've said it, too.

And sometimes it seems that way. Primarily because, like it or not, God is more committed to His own glory than to our comfort. And because that's true, He brings circumstances into our lives that seem, at the time, anything but good. Circumstances that squeeze us and stretch us and pull away from us the very things we think bring life! And in those dark moments, when our life's dream feels shattered, we say—like Naomi said—"It's God's fault. He could have done something . . . but He didn't."

But hang on: Naomi came back . . . when? Just as the harvest was beginning. Don't you dare dismiss that "coincidence." When Naomi was in her darkest despair, a new day was dawning in Bethlehem. Now she couldn't possibly know that, but God was just about to take her shattered dream and forge out something even greater.

As It Turned Out

"So she went out and began to glean in the fields behind the harvesters. As it turned out, she found herself working in a field belonging to Boaz, who was from the clan of Elimelech" (2:3).

That dream begins to reveal itself in the second passage I want you to see. Ruth had said to Naomi, "Let me go pick some grain." She didn't know where she was going—she was a foreigner! She just "accidentally" stumbled into the right place at the right time. Right. Are you kidding me? No way! Ruth stumbled onto that field by sovereign direction.

She was only interested in food—but God saw to it that she went to the right field. "As it turned out . . . as it turned out . . . !"

I wish I could tell you how many times God has done that same thing in my life. When I've felt forsaken, abandoned, desperate—when I couldn't imagine how I'd ever get out of my mess! Yet, as it turned out . . .

I'd shout, "God, why'd you bring me here only to hide from me and allow me all this heartache, all this unfair abuse and undeserved pain? God, I don't understand what You're trying to do to me!" I've said that! Yet, as it turned out . . .

My life a shambles, my calling taken from me, my very reason for breathing forever lost. Yet, as it turned out . . .

I tried, but couldn't conjure up even one exit strategy that would extricate me from all my madness! At the end of my rope—not another ounce of hope. Yet when it couldn't possibly get any worse—

As it turned out . . .

As it turned out, God was at work in my life! All along the way, at every crossroads of my journey, in every dark moment and every empty place—as it turned out . . . God was there!

That explains why Jesus was abandoned on the cross. When He said, "My God, my God, why have you forsaken me?" (Matthew 27:46) it was true—Jesus really was forsaken. We think it's true when we feel like God has left us. But Jesus *was* forsaken so we would never have to be. I know you feel otherwise—but you're wrong.

When He was abandoned on the cross, at that precise moment, the apostle Paul tells us, God was working through Christ to reconcile the world to himself. It wasn't senseless pain. It wasn't agony without a purpose.

And in your moment of agony, your time of pain? God is at work in you, too, working to create within you an even greater dream than the one you're so desperately scrambling to maintain.

Your son comes home stone-drunk with the car smashed—there's still a higher dream. Maybe it's not the story you wanted it to be, but that greater dream is one of the reasons God has given this moment to you.

When you put your mother in an Alzheimer's unit and she doesn't know who you are, when she says, "You look familiar. Do I know you?"—how many of you rise up in that moment and say, "God, in the middle of this heartache, I want to bear Your name well. I don't want to blame You. I don't want to harangue You. I don't want to charge You with neglect for not providing a cure, and I don't want to charge You with abuse because you have the power but won't use it. I want to see the next dream. I want to see what You have for me in this!"

My little sister, two weeks ago, was declared legally blind. She's a single mom, with no child support—and now she can't work. Yeah, she's been down. Really down. But she called the other day, and do you know what she said? "Steve, I'm finally beginning to look for God's plan in all this. I want to find His purpose—His new dream for me."

I said, "Beckie, when you find it, it will be a far better dream than even your shattered dream."

Because . . . as it turns out . . . that's just the way He works. Remember the *X* Factor? When I choose to "keep in step with the Spirit," it's amazing how things just *happen* to "turn out"!

Ruth had no idea, but picking leftovers in a barley field was where God would give her the new life she desired. To her, it was "as it turned out," but in Heaven, it was God at work. Look at Ruth 4:13: "So Boaz took Ruth and she became his wife. Then he went to her, and the LORD enabled her to conceive, and she gave birth to a son." They made their choices, and they followed the prescribed formula, but the results were "enabled" by the Lord.

The one who'd been enabling behind the scenes all along enabled once more. "As it turned out . . ."

But at first, it didn't appear it would "turn out" that way.

The third passage I want you to see is in chapter three. Naomi is talking to Ruth. Ruth has just met Boaz. Boaz has fallen in love and wants to marry Ruth, but there's just one problem—someone else has the right of first refusal. Boaz told Ruth, "Somebody else, by Jewish law, has the right to marry you. I can talk to him, but if he wants you—he gets you."

The Man Won't Rest

"Then Naomi said, 'Wait, my daughter, until you find out what happens. For the man will not rest until the matter is settled today'" (3:18).

Ruth comes back to Naomi upset, but Naomi is somehow finding a rejuvenation of her faith. "Wait," she says. Naomi knew that Boaz—hot-blooded, ready-to-get-busy man that he was— would no doubt get right on this little project, not resting until he had his solution . . . not to mention a new wife.

But there's a second meaning. Please don't miss it, because this man's work is all over this story.

"The man" could also refer to the Father. The Father in Heaven. You know . . . the one who has the power to bless you— even though He's not currently blessing you the way you'd like to be blessed? He's not indifferent. He's not unaware. No, He's hard at work, even now, to bring about in your life a dream far beyond any other dream you've ever known.

So what's He up to right now? Well, for one thing, He's preparing a place, remember? So He's definitely working. And He "will not rest until the matter is settled." So "do not let your hearts be troubled" (John 14:1). Because He's preparing a place.

At some point, friend, that's the place you've got to get to. At some point, you've got to realize that your bottom-line hope isn't connected to this world. That your place of happiness and your source of joy aren't wrapped up in what Jesus is doing for you now, but what He's going to do later when He takes you home. And *the man* is not going to rest . . . *The Man* is not going to rest . . . until the matter is settled.

So for now—sometimes the worst thing you can do is rush ahead and take on that shattered dream all by your lonesome. That's why Naomi said, "Wait, my daughter."

Just slow down. Don't race ahead. Don't knock down all those obstacles and turn all those doorknobs—because it might just be that behind that door is something that's not God's plan for you.

God's plan is that you wait, and *if* you wait it may just turn out—in fact, I can absolutely guarantee you it *will* turn out—that The Man has been working all along. Working out His perfect will. Forging out your new dream. Shaping and molding your life into exactly what He intends for you to be.

Dueling Tevyes. When I was in high school, our spring musical was *Fiddler on the Roof.* If you've ever seen that show, you know that the lead character is a big guy with an even bigger mouth. I mean, can there be any doubt? I was perfect for the part! And I'll be honest, I desperately wanted to be Tevye.

But there was another guy who also wanted to be Tevye. And he wanted the part so bad that he launched a smear campaign against me. He said some awful things about me—not only to other students but even to the faculty who would be casting the play. His attack was so vicious. He even tried to convince me that the tryout dates had been changed so that I wouldn't show up!

TRADING PLACES

Now I'm a pretty sensitive guy. And those attacks were really getting to me! To the point that I almost gave up. I came this close to throwing in the towel and letting good ol' Jim-bo have exactly what he wanted.

However, when our director found out I was considering surrender? He pulled me aside and said, "Steve, I really want you to try out. Do you hear me? You have to promise me—no matter how discouraged you get—promise me you will try out! Promise?"

I promised. And when I showed up for the tryouts—I sang the songs, I read the lines, and . . . doggone it, I got the part!

Fifteen years later, I stopped in to see my former director because I had a question. You see, in the years since *Fiddler,* having directed dozens of shows myself, I realized something I could never have known back then. I realized that my director knew all along that he was going to pick me. The truth is, he chose that musical with me in mind! That's why he made me promise! I asked him, "Mr. Penry, did you know all along you were gonna pick me?"

He said, "Of course! Steve, a good director never picks a show without first casting it in his mind."

Your divine director has chosen for you a special part to play. The trouble is, as you recite your lines and move through a sticky plot filled with all kinds of heartache and loss and unjust suffering, you tend to think, *I've got to do something!* Or like me, *I'm just gonna give up! This isn't ever gonna happen for me!*

And yet, all the while, the divine director is saying, "Listen child, I'm *The Man.* And I picked this play just for you. Every line, every twist, every setback—I chose it just for you. So don't walk away in disgust. Don't trash your playbook in anger. Just read the lines. Just follow the script.

"And please promise me something: promise me you'll wait for me to come through for you. Because I will. After all, I picked this story just for you."

The Father of David

"Then Naomi took the child, laid him in her lap and cared for him. The women living there said, 'Naomi has a son.' And they named him Obed. He was the father of Jesse, the father of David" (4:16, 17).

One last passage. The last verses I want you to see are the best of all.

Naomi now had a grandson, and boy, was she ready for that! The baby got a nanny, and Naomi found her story. The phrase "in her lap" is found only three times in Scripture. Each time it refers to an older person holding an infant, a baby who will continue the larger story of God long after that older person is dead.

You see, what Naomi needed to learn is what *we* need to learn. That it's not about me. We say to God, "Here's my life story just as I've drawn it up. And here's the deal, God. I will write, produce, direct, and star in this masterpiece—and all You've got to do is serve as my supporting cast. I mean, I'll do most of the heavy lifting. I just want You around to make sure everything runs smoothly. OK? You be my stagehand; I'll be the star!"

How does God respond to that? "No, that's not the way your story's going to be told. No, *I'm* the writer of your story, not you. And the producer . . . and the director. And guess what? My Son is the only star. Oh, you can play a bit part, but this story—even though it is your story—is not about you. No, your story—and her story and his story—everybody's story is ultimately all about my glory! And it's not about your comfort or your dreams, either. Because if I choose to use your suffering for my glory? It is what it is."

I picture Naomi, trying to remember what her husband looked like, straining to still hear her son's voice. But . . . she's holding a baby. And I hear her say, her eyes brimming with tears, "You know, I wish my son were here as the father of this child. But he's not; he's gone. But little Obed *is* here, right here in my lap. So I'm looking up. I'm understanding it now . . . I see it so clearly. There's more to life than me. There's a story being told, and God is using me to tell that story. I think I'll let Him."

Verse 17 is the verse I've waited pages to show you. It says that Ruth's baby boy, Obed, was the father of Jesse and the grandfather of Israel's King David. Now, I want you to get this. In Matthew 1 we find a listing of the genealogy of Jesus. In verse 2, the record begins with Abraham, and in verse 16 it concludes with "Joseph, the husband of Mary, of whom was born Jesus."

But somewhere in the middle of the unfolding of God's plan for redeeming man, when it seemed as though God wasn't there, that He certainly must not care . . . in verse 5, right there on that list is a man named Salmon who was—do you see it?—"the father of Boaz, whose mother was Rahab."

Then God sent a young Moabite woman who didn't know the end of the story—but God knew. And from their union Boaz became "the father of Obed, whose mother was Ruth." And "Obed . . . [was] the father of Jesse," and "Jesse [was] the father of King David" (vv. 5, 6). And so on and on—*until a tiny baby was laid in a manger and the story of God was finally revealed.*

Ruth was the great-grandmother of David. And all along, though Naomi didn't know it, Naomi's story was about paving a way for our Savior. Which means the famine and the death of her husband and the deaths of her sons—all the "bitterness" and sense of loss—every chapter, every line—all took place to tell, not Naomi's story, but God's story through Naomi.

Your story, His glory. I don't know where life has you right now. You may feel as though the story of your life is garbage—that life couldn't get any worse than it is right now. But why not take a look at you from the perspective of Heaven? I mean, what if God wrote in your script long ago that you would read this very book precisely because it's the "beginning of harvest" again? Could it be? That's why you've got to resist every temptation to charge ahead, and instead, you've got to "wait."

Or maybe life for you is turning around. Things really are—as it turns out—beginning to look up. It's finally your turn for good times, right? Time for things to roll your way for a change. But could it be that The Man—the producer, the divine director, and the only true star of your life—is actually hard at work, right now, behind the scenes of your life . . . bringing about His perfect will in you?

And could it be that if you just hold on and trust God's heart—if you glue yourself to His perfect purpose for you—maybe, just maybe, His blessings will fall right into your lap?

"He who promised is faithful," the Bible says (Hebrews 10:23). He is loyal to you—and hard at work on your behalf.

Not for your comfort, but for His glory.

So be like Ruth and Naomi and trade all that sorrow and all that loneliness and all that heartache for a bit part in an unfolding drama called *God at Work in You.* Because it may be your story, but it's not about you.

That's their story, folks. Two lonely women who chose loyalty over their loneliness. And because they did, their lives were forever changed—and God has preserved their story to help us write our own.

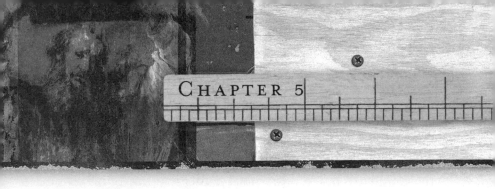

CHAPTER 5

TRADING REJECTION
FOR ROYALTY

THE NEWS CONFERENCE was scheduled for Wednesday, but it happened Tuesday instead. It was supposed to be about a proud father watching his son sign to play football for the Miami Hurricanes. Instead, it was a gaunt and tearful Walter Payton, barely resembling the durable, tough-as-nails superstar fans had always known. "An American icon withering away" is how one commentator described him.

Payton charged right into the belly of his bad news, just as he once charged through an opponent's front four, announcing that he had a rare liver disease and, unless he received a transplant, he would most certainly die.

The news resounded like a thunderclap. At the time, Walter was the NFL's all-time rushing leader. He'd been named to the Pro Bowl nine times. He led the Bears to a Super Bowl win in 1985, and in 1993 was inducted into the Pro Football Hall of Fame.

Yet on February 2, 1999, "Sweetness" wore a jacket to hide his dramatic weight loss and sunglasses to cover the jaundice in his once-sparkling eyes. His cheeks were hollow, his voice was hoarse, and his once powerful physique—a mere shadow.

As if losing his physical prowess wasn't enough, rumors were circulating, suggesting his weight loss was due to drug use or perhaps even AIDS. In anger, Payton hastily called the press conference "to set the record straight."

What made this news so stunning was that Payton was always the epitome of health. He trained harder than any of his teammates to stay in top condition—continuing that regimen even after hanging up his cleats. His teammates said he was invincible. His coach, Mike Ditka, called him "the best-conditioned athlete I've ever seen."

Yet, there he sat—the man who once vaulted goal lines and stiff-armed would-be tacklers—now feeble, fragile, and afraid.

Walter Payton . . . afraid?

"Yeah, I'm scared! Wouldn't you be? But what can I do? It's not in my hands. I'm in God's hands. I'm just doing what my mama told me to do. She said, 'Put it in God's hands, baby.' And since I've done that? It's been such a relief."

Nine months later, Walter Payton was gone. Coach Ditka said what the rest of us couldn't say: "This young man was the epitome of conditioning and strength. He was a rock. To have your body deteriorate like that right before your eyes and you can't stop it, well, it's not only mind boggling, it makes you pretty much aware that we're all vulnerable."[1]

You bet it does.

ROCKS AND HARD PLACES

Such things are supposed to happen to smokers and drinkers and couch potatoes. But a finely tuned instrument like Walter Payton? The deal we all bank on is: eat right, get a modicum of exercise, get eight hours of sleep—and your body will never, ever turn on you. Right? Wrong. Sometimes, like it or not, you end up in a place you never thought you'd be.

A young woman I know is a fitness freak and watches everything she eats, yet she has cancer.

A mom I know raised her children to follow Jesus, yet one of those kids is wandering. Sometimes mom goes to church, and she wonders what people think of her; she worries about what they say about her.

A husband is involved in a marital journey that is extremely hard. He's a good man, but his home is a place of desperation.

I've got hundreds of stories like that—stories far less well known than Payton's story—but all of them equally tragic.

My question for you is: what do you do when it happens to you? When *you* are the one who is rejected, when it's *your* health that's lost, when the child *you* love goes bad? When even though you live in the shadow of the cross and think your highest purpose is to bring glory to God, God has decided that, for whatever reason, you've got to stumble through some rocks and hard places.

I wonder: when it's your turn to pass through those rocky corridors—what do you do?

During his presidential campaign in 1960, John Kennedy delivered a speech at The Alamo. Now The Alamo is a memorial to the brave Texans who tried in vain to stand against an overpowering Mexican army.

After the speech, Kennedy was scheduled to make a hasty exit. Turning to one of the local politicians, he said, "I've got to get out of here. Where's the back door?"

The local replied, "Senator, if there had been a back door in The Alamo, there wouldn't have been any heroes."

And he's right. So what do you do? When you're in a dark place—and you want to get out of that place—but there's no back door? You're trapped; there's no way out. What *do* you do?

TALK ABOUT THE PITS

The Old Testament story of Joseph gives us some clues. When you're in a place you never thought you'd be; when you've been disappointed and mistreated, falsely accused and unfairly punished; when you've been forgotten and rejected, Joseph's story is a powerful reminder that even though you may not realize it, God is with you . . . and He will see you through.

Now it may not seem like it at the time.

Joseph, after all, was a good kid. Maybe too good, because he was obviously Dad's favorite—a truth that really ticked off his brothers. Talk about feeling rejected—they tossed Joseph into a pit, sold him to some traveling salesmen headed for Egypt—then told Dad he'd been eaten by a wild animal!

Upon arrival in Egypt, Joseph was sold as a slave to a henchman named Potiphar. Are you tracking Joseph's rapid descent? Once the favored son, now a flunky slave. That's rejection #2!

If that's not bad enough? After he wins Potiphar's favor and launches an actual career path with a promising future, Mrs. Potiphar puts the moves on him! She tries to seduce him. And when he doesn't go along? She falsely accuses Joseph of rape, and he gets plopped in the pokey. Hurled in the hoosegow. Stuck in the slammer. Bounced into the big house. (Sorry.) But that's major rejection #3.

Now don't you figure Joseph had just about had it? He'd been dumped in a dungeon! (I can't seem to quit.) You've got to know he wondered, *What's up, God? This is ridiculous!*

To Joseph's credit, while cooling it in the cooler (OK, I'll stop.), he befriended Pharaoh's cupbearer who was also imprisoned. He even interpreted the cupbearer's dream on the condition that once the cupbearer was released—as Joseph correctly predicted—he'd seek Joseph's release, too. But the cupbearer didn't do that. He forgot all about Joseph. Are you keeping count? That's monumental rejection #4.

Don't kid yourself: Joseph struggled with all four. He was in a place he never thought he'd be—a place he didn't deserve to be—yet, as we'll see, these apparently negative experiences were actually God's way of preparing Joseph for his assignment of a lifetime.

The day would come when Joseph would rise to second in command over the most powerful nation on earth—trading in rejection for royalty! And what I want you to see from his story is that every one of those agonizing rejections led Joseph to exactly where God wanted him to be—and helped him become the person God needed him to be.

And I want you to see that maybe, just maybe, that's why *you* are in your dark place, too.

GOD WAS "WITH" JOSEPH

Now *we* know, because we can read the story, there was never a moment when God wasn't near Joseph. Four times in Genesis 39 alone we read, "The LORD was with Joseph." I'm sure Joseph felt alone, but he wasn't. He may have thought he was abandoned, but God was always by his side.

That may sound comforting—but I wonder if Joseph felt like the old codger who, as he lay dying, turned to his wife and whispered, "When I limped home from the War in 1918, you were waiting for me, Rachel. When I was released from Dachau at the end of World War II, you were by my side."

Overcome with emotion, he snorted into his handkerchief, then continued, "Rachel, when we sold everything to start a business and it went bust and left us penniless, there you were. And now, here I am breathing my last, and here you still stand by my bedside. Rachel, I'm telling you—you're a *jinx!*"

You think maybe Joseph went there, too? Maybe he would have agreed with Tevye in *Fiddler on the Roof:* "Dear God, it's true that we are the Chosen People. But once in a while, can't you choose someone else?"[2]

Can't you just hear Joseph telling God, "I appreciate You hangin' around and all, but could You find someone else to be 'with'?"

If Joseph had such feelings, they probably reached their climax when he interpreted the cupbearer's dream. He did so with just one request: "When all goes well with you, remember me . . . ; mention me to Pharaoh and get me out of this prison" (Genesis 40:14).

However . . .

"The chief cupbearer, however, did not remember Joseph; he forgot him" (v. 23).

FORGOTTEN!

Three days later, and Joseph was forgotten. Fact is, Joseph pined away in that prison not for two more days or two more weeks or even two more months. Genesis 41:1 says it was two more years!

Now a day seems like an eternity when people are speculating you might have AIDS. And an hour seems like infinity when the Mexicans are shooting and there's no back door. But two full years? For a crime you didn't commit?

But that's the story: for two years the screen goes blank, no lines are written, just the slow-moving grind of a life on hold.

Now that's not true. That's our perspective. It was probably even Joseph's perspective. But the truth is, God was accomplishing things in Joseph's life during those two years that could not be accomplished any other way. He was preparing him, tooling him, training him for an assignment yet before him.

TRADING PLACES

The world's most famous bad-luck guy, Job, expressed the same emotions Joseph must have felt. Broken and bruised, haunted by the death of his kids and the loss of his home, his career, and even his health, Job had lost everything, and he was ticked off! He said of the Lord, "If only I knew where to find him; if only I could go to his dwelling! I would state my case before him and fill my mouth with arguments" (Job 23:3, 4).

"Because I've got questions," Job is saying. "The biggest being, *Why?* Why did You do this?"

"But if I go to the east, he is not there; if I go to the west, I do not find him. When he is at work in the north, I do not see him; when he turns to the south, I catch no glimpse of him" (vv. 8, 9).

What God's up to, I have no clue. Where He's at, I do not know! What He sees, I'm cannot see! But I know this:

"He knows the way that I take; when he has tested me, I will come forth as gold" (v. 10).

The key word is *when.* When He has finished preparing me, that's when this will end. When God says "when." And not one minute before.

There's no such thing as instant gold. Refining, purifying, and perfecting gold is a lengthy, painstaking process. And God is telling us, through Job, that affliction and pain—that time alone in a dungeon and life lived in the pits—is gold in the making for the child of God.

And He alone determines the number of ticks on the clock. Or the *X*s on your calendar. He alone is the one who says "when."

For Joseph it was two full years.

DREAM WEAVER

His big moment came on a day like any other day. Except on this day, an angel probably said, "God, is Joseph soup yet?"

"Yep, he's soup. It's 'when,' folks! 'When' has come. It's time for my golden boy to do what I've prepared him to do. Pharaoh, do the dream."

And what a dream it was! Pharaoh dreamed he was standing by the Nile, when seven skinny cows came along and swallowed seven fat cows. Then he had another dream about seven scrawny heads of grain swallowing up seven healthy heads of grain.

The Bible says "his mind was troubled, so he sent for all the magicians and wise men of Egypt" (Genesis 41:8).

Now "magicians" doesn't refer to some ancient David Blaine type, but to soothsayers. Astrologers. You know, the dot-com doctors of dreamology?

"Pharaoh told them his dreams, but no one could interpret them" (v. 8). They had no clue what those dreams meant! Do you know why? They were God's dreams—so only God could interpret them.

As news spread through the palace, the cupbearer was instantly seized with guilt. He said to Pharaoh, "Today I am reminded of my shortcomings. Pharaoh was once angry with his servants, and he imprisoned me and the chief baker. . . . Each of us had a dream the same night, and each dream had a meaning of its own. Now a young Hebrew was there with us, a servant of the captain of the guard. We told him our dreams, and he interpreted them for us" (vv. 9-12).

Isn't it amazing how God wove the tapestry of Joseph's life? Events happening years before now culminated in this singularly powerful moment when the cupbearer said, "Pharaoh, I can't believe I forgot, but . . .

"Things turned out exactly as he interpreted them" (v. 13).

Pharaoh replies, "Well . . . go get him!"

Meanwhile, Joseph is clueless. He's in the dungeon lifting weights, watching *American Idol*—when all of a sudden, *rattle, clang, squeak!* He's free! They clean him up, give him some fresh duds, and like a flash, that favored-son-turned-slave-boy-turned-ex-con has an audience with the king of Egypt!

You know who else was there? The cupbearer. The man solely responsible for two years of Joseph's misery! Yet there's no hint that Joseph even considered revenge. Now it could have been payback time—"Your Highness, I'll interpret your dream, but you get rid of Bozo first! Deal?"

Joseph didn't do that. Do you know why?

Because Joseph had begun to sense that God was using this circumstance to prepare him. That this "rejection"—which was yet another in a long line of rejections—was, in truth, actually God's hidden training program. So instead of whining, saying, "Why me?" Joseph patiently waited for God's "when."

"Pharaoh said to Joseph, 'I had a dream, and no one can interpret it. But I have heard . . . that when you hear a dream you can interpret it'" (v. 15).

I hear you're the dream weaver!

Joseph said, "I cannot do it, . . . but God will give Pharaoh the answer he desires" (v. 16).

Talk about integrity. I mean, this was Joseph's chance! He could have said anything and gotten away with it! "That's right, Pharaoh, I *am* the dream weaver. And if that Bozo over there hadn't forgotten me? I could have been weaving your dreams for two years by now!"

Or he could have said, "I'll do your dream. On one condition: I want a loaded camel, plenty o' shekels, and safe passage to Canaan! Deal?"

From a purely human vantage point, Joseph was the man! But after thirteen years of daily depending on God and discovering that his only hope was in "waiting for" God, Joseph wasn't about to make this "all about me."

Instead, "Pharaoh, I don't have the answers you need. But there is a God who lives far beyond the stars your soothsayers study. In fact, my God can take a star and hold it in His hand! He's the one who'll tell you about your dreams!"

Pharaoh told him all about the cows and the grain. And in verse 25, Joseph said, "[Your] dreams . . . are one and the same. God has revealed to Pharaoh what he is about to do.

"The seven good cows are seven years, and the seven good heads of grain are seven years. . . . The seven lean, ugly cows that came up afterward are seven years, and so are the seven worthless heads of grain . . . : They are seven years of famine" (vv. 26, 27).

"What's going to happen, Pharaoh," Joseph was saying, "is that Egypt will have seven years of a bumper crop followed by seven years of famine. A famine so intense, it will ravage the land."

"The reason the dream was given to Pharaoh in two forms is that the matter has been firmly decided by God, and God will do it soon" (v. 32).

Can't you hear Joseph saying, "This is a done deal, King. And it's going to happen—*soon!*"

Do you see the recurring theme? *God* is doing this! It's not me, it's Him!

See, Joseph had Traded Places a long time ago! It started in the pit, was confirmed at Potiphar's place, and was absolutely tattooed on his heart in that dungeon.

Joseph knew the source of his power. The wings he soared on weren't his wings—this was a God thing!

Joseph adds one final piece of advice: "And now let Pharaoh look for a discerning and wise man and put him in charge of the land of Egypt" (v. 33).

I can imagine Joseph elaborating: "You're going to have to implement a strategic plan. You're going to have to ration food during the good years in order to have enough food during the bad years. And someone will need to direct that operation! He'll have to design and build huge granaries where all that food can be stored. And also develop a plan for distribution. You need a good lieutenant, sir!"

Do you know what impresses me about that? Not once does Joseph say, "And here I am, reporting for duty, sir!" He doesn't grease the skids, he doesn't capitalize on this crisis in some attempt to advance his own agenda, and he doesn't try to "assist" God— he just says, "Make sure you get the right man."

"The plan seemed good to Pharaoh and to all his officials. So Pharaoh asked them, 'Can we find anyone like this man, one in whom is the spirit of God?'" (vv. 37, 38).

Evidently, these two enjoyed an almost instant connection.

Like the one between Ben and Jerry of Ben & Jerry's Ice Cream. Jerry writes:

> We met at junior high school in seventh grade when we were the two slowest, fattest kids running around the track together. Coach Phelps was yelling at us, "Gentlemen, you've got to run the mile in under seven minutes. If you don't run the mile in under seven minutes, you're going to have to do it again."
>
> And there were Ben and I in this little pack way behind the rest of the pack. Ben yelled, "Gee coach, if I don't run it in under seven minutes the first time, I'm certainly not going to run it in under seven minutes the second time."
>
> Jerry said, "That's when I realized Ben was someone I wanted to get to know."[3]

Same thing here. It was instant affinity as Pharaoh realized, *Joseph's got the goods to do this!* So he said, "Since God has made all this known to you, there is no one so discerning and wise as you" (v. 39).

GOD HELP US

Now Pharaoh's doing it! Pharaoh doesn't say, "Joseph, you're unbelievable!" He says, "Since God helped you do the dream, maybe He'll help us save Egypt!"

That's when finally—after rejection piled upon heartache followed by extreme loss—*finally* it's promotion time! It's "when," Joseph! God said "when!"

"You shall be in charge of my palace," Pharaoh said, "and all my people are to submit to your orders. Only with respect to the throne will I be greater than you. . . . I hereby put you in charge of the whole land of Egypt" (vv. 40, 41).

If you didn't know better, you might think this was Joseph's lucky day! Finally! The dude caught a break, right? I can see the pop-up ads now: "From Prison Cell to Pharaoh's Court! How I achieved greatness and how you can, too!" But that's not the story.

Joseph had fallen, and he wasn't getting up. He couldn't get up! But God lifted him up. And that's when Joseph realized: every potentially harmful experience in his life—God had used for good! Including his brothers, Mrs. Potiphar, the cupbearer . . . everybody! Events that seemed, at the time, totally unrelated—and entirely senseless—were now linked together into a marvelous chain of events, all leading Joseph to a place he never could have conceived. But God did.

May I share with you three things I've learned from this story?

Ask Who, Not Why

I've learned that when you're in a place you never thought you'd be, when your back is to the wall and there's no way out, there is no more popular—nor less productive—question in all the world than *why?*

A dad raced across town to watch his son's track meet. He hurriedly parked the car, and in his rush to watch his boy, he inadvertently wandered onto the shot-put range.

Spectators tried to warn him, but when he paused to see what they were shouting about, he got bonked on the head by a 16-pound shot! Later, when he regained consciousness, his first two words were, "Why me?"

Of course. It's what we all ask. But asking why is like pulling one leg off a centipede—it doesn't get you anywhere.

Why? It's a question that constantly taunts us. Because *why* rarely finds its answer. For every "why?" the answer is "because," and for every "because" there's another "why?"

If you don't believe me, tell a three-year-old she can't have a cookie!

I find it intriguing that Joseph never asks that question. Tossed into a pit and left for dead, yet no "Why me?" is found. Unfairly charged with a crime he didn't commit, yet not one chorus of "Why won't God do something?" Imprisoned and forgotten, betrayed and abandoned, yet no "Why is everybody always pickin' on me?"

And do you know why? Because the right question to ask in the face of heartache is not "why?"; it's "who?" "Who is involved in this?" There are three possible answers:

Them, the people around me who caused my pain, and who don't seem to care that I'm *in* pain.

Or . . .

Him, meaning God.

Or . . .

Me, the target of all this abuse and the only one in control of my responses.

Them. Let's deal with them first. Since it's obvious we can't control what *they* do, it's useless to waste time focusing on them, right? Or to expect anything from them. So if other people are the source of your pain, learn to give up your need to expect even the least bit of change from them. That's a spiritual cul-de-sac, leading absolutely nowhere.

Yeah, Joseph should have been able to trust his brothers. He should have been able to count on his cell mate. But rather than carp and complain about it, Joseph realized what *we* need to realize: when you're in a place you'd rather not be, there are only two points of focus that will help you—Him and me.

Him. Let's deal with the Him part. To the question "Who is my ultimate hope?" the answer, obviously, is Him. God!

So while dinkin' around in the dungeon, Joseph rehearsed everything he knew about God: that God was too kind to hurt him and too wise to make a mistake.

And that God was his only hope for deliverance. So rather than hammer away at "why . . . why . . . why?"—instead of blaming God and getting ticked at God—Joseph asked the "who" question and put his trust in Him—the only "Him" who could truly deliver.

Me. The last part of the "who" question is me. "What do I do with all of my confusion? . . . What do I do when answers won't come and God seems so far away? . . . When I can't do anything but just passively wait for Him to provide His rescue? And what do I do when it doesn't come? When it's not *when* yet? What do *I* do?"

Sadly, most often I slip back into asking "why" questions. I doubt God's goodness and I question His love. I ask, "Why did God let this happen to me?" when what I should ask is, "How can I use this for His glory and my good?" That's the only question that brings healing!

Like it or not—and I don't—British pastor and author Alan Redpath was right when he said, "When God wants to do an impossible task, He takes an impossible person and crushes him."

Yet "he knows the way that I take; when he has tested me, I will come forth as gold" (Job 23:10). And when I choose to believe that when I unconditionally commit myself to the inevitability of God's rightful plan for me, then I live life anchored to the bedrock of what I know to be true—regardless of how I may feel or how difficult the circumstance.

So rather than harass God with a bunch of "whys," I'm learning to look to Him as my help, to look inside for *my* correct response, and to look ahead to the character development and greater use He has planned for me. I put off my need to know why and put on a confident and abiding spirit of hope.

Don't you see? It's not the why that's going to anchor my life anyway. It's the who!

Waiting, Not Wrestling

I've also learned that dungeon experiences are not a time for wrestling, but for waiting. It's not a season for great debate, but rather for the Great Exchange!

Thirteen years is a long time, especially when it's filled with unkept promises, undeserved rejection, and—can you believe we're talking about it again?—interminable delay.

But as I read my Bible, I've yet to find even one significant Bible hero who didn't spend at least some time in God's waiting room.

The problem is, you and I consider waiting time to be wasted time; but in God's economy, waiting time is training time.

Remember the movie *Karate Kid*? Daniel wants to learn karate from Mr. Miyagi. He shows up for his first lesson and there are a half dozen cars lined up. Miyagi hands him some soap and wax and says, "First, wash cars, all of them. Then wax."

What for?

"Uhh! Wax on . . . right hand. Wax off . . . left hand. Wax on . . . wax off."

The next day it's, "Sand deck. Right circle. Left circle. Whole deck."

Daniel's frustrated, but he really wants to learn karate. So the next day he comes back.

This time it's, "Paint fence. Wrist up . . . wrist down." And then, "Paint house—side to side."

About that time, Daniel blew a cork! He says, "You're not teaching me karate; I'm your stinkin' slave! It's been four days and it's nothing but 'sand deck,' 'wax car,' 'paint house!'"

Mr. Miyagi replies, "Things are not as seem. Show me 'sand floor.' Show me 'wax on, wax off.' Show me 'paint fence.'"

And all of a sudden, it became so clear. He *had* been learning karate moves all along. Those four days weren't wasted days; they were training days—and Daniel hadn't even realized it.

Neither did Joseph. How could he? To see those thirteen years as training? All designed to prepare him for the task that now lay before him? How could he have known?

We don't get it, either. We live in such an instant age that everything has to fit inside a microwave or a sixty-minute TV drama. A twenty-minute oil change is too slow! Waiting to start my car after I'm inside is a waste of time. I need remote ignition!

Yet it takes time to shape a saint. It's worth every minute you're on hold if it means that in the process you're being groomed for God's greater plan.

The Bible says, "Wait for the LORD, and keep His way, and He will exalt you" (Psalm 37:34, NASB). So Joseph waited in the pit, and sure enough, God shaped him for the palace.

And it's in the pit where He wants to shape you, too. "Are you sayin' God's trying to teach me something through my messed up life?" Duh! God's *always* trying to teach you something! You are His lifetime student, pal, and you will never graduate.

So stop wrestling . . . and learn the blessed peace found in simply waiting for Him.

Promise, Not Promotion

I've also learned to stop begging for promotion and, instead, start believing God's promise.

There are two ways to get a promotion. One way is to exalt yourself. And Joseph could have done that. "Pharaoh, you need a guy like me on your team because everything I touch turns to gold, baby. Trust me . . . I'm the man for this job!"

The second way to get a promotion is to put someone else down. Joseph could have done that, too. "Pharaoh, I could have helped you out of jams for two years now, if it hadn't been for Cleo the Cup-bearer over there! Give me the ball and I'll run like Walter Payton!"

But he didn't do that, either. Joseph didn't bargain, he didn't connive, he didn't scheme.

PIT-STOP THEOLOGY

Listen, there's something about waiting in a pit that teaches a teachable person to abandon any and all conspiracies—whether you're trying to advance yourself or hinder another. Joseph learned the hard way—God didn't need his help. And He doesn't need yours, either.

I've got a promise from God for you to hang onto. "Humble yourselves, therefore, under God's mighty hand, that he may lift you up in due time. Cast all your anxiety on him because he cares for you. . . . And the God of all grace, who called you to his eternal glory in Christ, after you have suffered a little while, will himself restore you and make you strong, firm and steadfast" (1 Peter 5:6, 7, 10).

That's God's promise. When you've fallen and can't get up? "In due time" He'll lift you up. It doesn't say "in no time" but "in due time." In God's time. When God says "when."

"When and how" is His job, and only He can do it. He doesn't need your help. He doesn't need scheming power brokers or black-market transplants.

What He needs from you is what Walter's mama told him to do: He needs you to humble yourself and put this thing in God's hands, baby. Even when your heart is breaking and you're not sure you can take one more rejection, you need to cast all your anxiety on Him.

But whatever you do, stop trying to rush the process! Stop trying to the pick the locks on your prison bars! Stop trying to exalt yourself or put someone else down! Instead, just rest in God's *promise!* Remember the Great Exchange!

When ESPN's Bob Ley interviewed Payton, he said, "Walter, you set the all-time rushing record, and now you're an accomplished businessman. In those two venues, you make your own decisions. But this seems out of your hands. Do you feel uneasy about that?"

Payton said, "Well, certain things you have control over and certain things you don't. . . . It's like you're standing up there looking at a track that has twenty miles on it. You say, 'Well, I can make that twenty miles if I prepare myself.' But you can never prepare yourself for the obstacles along the way. That's where everything goes back into God's hands."

Wow. Walter's mama is right. Puttin' it in God's hands really is about all you *can* do, isn't it?

Maybe you're in the pits right now. And it's dark down there. But what you don't realize is that you might—right now—be on the verge of God's promotion. You just don't know it because God doesn't announce promotions. They just happen. "In due time," remember?

I can personally bear testimony to you that the God who made that promise is faithful—and He *will* deliver. So if you want to trade rejection for royalty, you've got to start by humbling yourself, OK?

Our world is chock full of broken, bitter people—simply because their dreams were shattered, their plans up-ended, their passions put on hold.

But Joseph has taught me that . . .

if I allow God to be the *who* that controls my life;

if I'll just stop wrestling and trust in His perfect timing;

if I'll just quit begging for what I think I deserve and wait instead for His unconditional promise . . .

then my life will far exceed my dreams.

In Lynn Anderson's *Shepherd's Song,* a wise man asks, "Isn't God smart enough to know the best use of my life?" That's a great question . . . and if the answer is yes—if it's true that God is smart enough to know the best use of my life—then maybe I need to trust Him.

CHAPTER 6

TRADING WHINING FOR WINNING

IT WAS THE MOST BEAUTIFUL golf course I'd ever seen. My friends and I had gotten a tee time at the Pelican Hill Golf Club in Newport Beach, California. Our car was parked by a valet, my clubs were polished by young boys in matching outfits, and our group had just been called by the announcer. And there I was—up to the red tee, ready to swing—when suddenly the speakers blared, "Would the man at the red tee please step back to the white tee?"

I looked up sheepishly, then resumed my stance and readied my swing.

Again the announcer said, "Would the man at the red tee please step back to the white tee?" and added, "The red tees are for women only."

I was so humiliated! I stepped back, looked around, and resumed my stance.

By now the announcer was ticked! "Would somebody *please* tell the man at the red tee to step back to the white tee?"

Totally exasperated, I shouted back, "Would someone please tell the PA announcer that I'm on my second shot?"

Geesh! It's really embarrassing to hear your mess-up—your little dribble off the tee—broadcast to the entire English-speaking world!

I'll be honest. I was thinking, *Can I puhleeez have a mulligan?* I just wanted to pick up my ball, walk back to the white tee, and start over. I wanted a mulligan!

Need a mulligan?

Now if you've played a few rounds in another game called Real Life, you know there comes a time when everybody wants to start over.

Sometimes that's because you're in a sand trap someone else put you in, as in the case of Joseph. Other times you did it right like Ruth, choosing to remain loyal to Naomi. Yet she still paid a price, didn't she?

But more often than not, you tend to need mulligans because you royally messed up! You sliced the ball . . . big time. And now you look around at all the chaos you've caused, and wonder, *Will my life ever be the same? Will I ever get to start over again?*

You may find this hard to believe, but if that's where you are, please know that no less a man of God than Moses wondered the exact same thing.

You'll remember that baby Moses escaped Pharaoh's death sentence when he was dredged out of the Nile. And though he was a Hebrew, Moses was raised as Egyptian royalty . . . and was, many believe, in direct line for the throne.

But Moses never forgot his roots. He always believed that his life had been saved so that, someday, he could save others—specifically, the Hebrews, by leading them out of bondage.

Fast-forward forty years. Israel has been in bondage for three hundred years now. They're living like slaves, functioning as cheap labor for a pyramid-crazy king. Moses is now fully grown—and still driven by a passion to free his people and grab

God's great vision for his life. The only trouble is, he jumps the gun a bit.

The Bible says he decided one day to go out and watch the Hebrews at "hard labor" (see Exodus 2:11 and Acts 7:23). Note that *he* decided. He didn't get this from God; he made this call all by his lonesome.

Because Moses had a dream, right? And he was raised to believe his dreams would come true! Acts 7:20 says that even from birth it was obvious—Moses was "no ordinary child."

For one thing, he was handsome! So handsome that Josephus, an ancient Jewish historian, tells us that the Egyptians would wait outside the palace just to catch a glimpse of him!

He was also strong, so strong he killed an Egyptian with only his bare hands, as far as we know (see Exodus 2:12).

He was also intellectually gifted, having received the finest education in the most advanced culture of his day.

Even more, as the son of Pharaoh's daughter, Moses surely must have believed that one day *he* might be pharaoh!

So when "he saw an Egyptian beating a Hebrew" (Exodus 2:11), this proud, strong, highly gifted, and well-trained leader—looking and feeling a lot like Arnold Schwarzenegger—said to the Egyptian, "*Hasta la vista,* baby!"

EVERY WHICH WAY BUT UP

What do you do when you're about to do something you shouldn't? Don't you look around to see if anyone is watching? That's what Moses did next. "Glancing this way and that and seeing no one . . ." (Exodus 2:12). Moses looked left and he looked right, but he never looked *up*. He made sure the coast was clear horizontally, but he never checked for clearance vertically.

TRADING PLACES

He just did a little looky-lou and then "killed the [guy] and hid him in the sand" (v. 12).

Why did he do it? Because he "thought that his own people would realize that God was using him to rescue them" (Acts 7:25). Somehow, somewhere along the way, God had convinced him: "Moses, you're my deliverer!" So Moses sees this Hebrew getting his bell rung and thinks, *This is it. This is my moment. After all, I'm forty . . . not getting any younger. Let's get ready to rumble!*

Have you ever run ahead of God's plan?

You want to be married, so you contrive to get a mate—even though he's obviously not God's choice for you.

You need more income, so you take a new job—without ever looking up to see if that job is where you ought to be.

Sometimes it's fear that drives us, sometimes it's pride, sometimes it's the very best of intentions, but we charge ahead without God's green light. And then, when the whole deal blows sky-high, we carp and complain, we bellyache and we blame—everybody and everything but ourselves!

When the truth is, the problem is . . . *us.* We're trying to do God's will, but we insist on doing it our way.

Moses' heart was right. His motives were genuine. But instead of waiting for God to open the door, Moses charged right in and blew it!

The next day when two Hebrews were fighting, he discovered how much he blew it. He stepped in, saying, "Uh, excuse me. You may not recognize me, but I'm . . . God's deliverer." But they didn't happen to want to be delivered, especially not by Moses! So they bristled.

"Who made you ruler and judge over us? Are you thinking of killing me as you killed the Egyptian?" (Exodus 2:14).

When Moses heard this, he was afraid. So afraid that he got out of Dodge, baby! Acts 7:29 says "he fled." Which was a good thing because when Pharaoh heard the news? He put a bounty on Moses' head.

MARATHON TO MIDIAN

So Moses ran and ran till he came to an obscure village on the backside of the desert. And every step of the way, I think Moses' self-doubt absolutely raged in his heart! This was the most colossal failure of his life! No wonder he ran! Till finally, Exodus 2:15 says, he "went to live in Midian, where he sat down by a well."

Plopped is probably a better word. Because the juice was gone, folks! Everything he'd lived for and worked for was lost. The strong, educated, handsome, capable Moses—the involved, busy, active leader Moses—was reduced to sitting. Sittin' on a rock by the well . . . wasting time. At the end of his rope . . . at the bottom of the barrel . . . Sittin' on a rock by the well.

In the movie *The Kid,* a guy named Russ is visited by an eight-year-old version of himself, a kid named Rusty. After they assure each other that they are, in fact, each other, Rusty starts quizzing Russ about his life. When he discovers Russ doesn't have a dog, he says:

"No dog? I grow up to be a guy with no dog?"

"Yeah."

"What do I do?" the kid asks.

"You're an image consultant," says the elder.

The kid takes inventory. "So . . . I'm forty, I'm not married, I don't fly jets, and I don't have a dog? I grow up to be a loser!?" That's Moses. All that promise, all that incredible potential . . . sitting by a well.

STONE-SITTING

Now "sit" isn't all Moses did. All told, he spent forty years in Midian. So, ultimately, life would go on. Moses established a new career as a hireling tending stinky sheep! He started a family. But I think the phrase that most marked those forty years was "he sat down by a well."

I think that every time Moses went to that well, he plopped down on that rock, and with tears streaming down his face, he'd rehearse his failure. Once an Egyptian prince, now a lowly shepherd. Once a resident of the palace, now a tenement dweller. Once a place at Pharaoh's table, now eating dust in the desert.

Can you imagine? Instead of using that stone to rest, he used it to beat himself up! Rehearsing every shortcoming and every failure. Wishing that the hands on the clock could roll back so he'd have a second chance.

Have you ever sat on a stone like that?

You wish for your 20s back because you were so wasted you hardly remember them.

You wish you hadn't broken your wedding vows . . . or lied to your client . . . or visited that hooker.

You wish you'd never visited that porn site or tried that dope.

I realize some of you are so wearied by life that the thought of forty years on a rock sounds almost like a much-needed vacation. And nudging sheep around the desert sounds like a very attractive career move!

Think again, pal. Every day, all day, Moses had to confront the ugly reality of his failure, not to mention the unresolved guilt of having let God down. For forty years, Moses lived with regret. Aarrrggghhh! No wonder he "sat down."

This is a good place to pause and underscore a singularly significant truth: failure is not a crime, but failure to learn from failure is. See, the difference between the best of us and the rest of us is not the number of mistakes we make but rather, do we wallow in them or rise above? Do we admit our failures and learn from them, or do we go to great lengths to keep them under wraps?

It's not *if* you make mistakes. That's a given. It's what you do after you make a mistake that matters. Sadly, most of our efforts to distance ourselves from our mistakes tend instead to forever bond us to our failure! We're our own worst enemies when we blow it, primarily because we don't like to look foolish. We work real hard not to lose face. So rather than learning from our failure and moving on, we just wallow in the stuff!

WAYS TO WALLOW

May I mention some ways we tend to do that?

First, *we cover it over.* Like Moses tried to bury the Egyptian he killed, we try to bury our sin. We deny it—to ourselves . . . and others. We construct expensive, elaborate disguises. We build a labyrinth of supporting lies and deceptions just to hide the one big lie.

But no matter how clever we are, no matter how we try to circumvent the truth, the deception can last only so long. Eventually, the truth *will* come out! (See 1 Peter 2:23 and Hebrews 10:30.)

Moses buried the Egyptian in the sand, but evidently he couldn't even get that right! One preacher jokingly suggested, "He left the toes out!"

And that's the way it is with failure. For a while you can ignore the crisis. You can pretend it didn't happen. You can tell yourself that everything will be just fine. But if you don't learn the lessons failure is meant to teach you, then like Moses, you could be sitting by a well for a long, long time.

We also deal with failure by *spreading it around.* Sometimes the failure is so obvious, it can't be denied. So we try the next approach; namely, finger someone else and blame them.

The boss blames his staff, marketing blames research, the teacher blames his student. The child blames his parent. The parent blames the child. It's "anybody but me, baby!"

No doubt Moses had his list, too. He blamed Pharaoh for mistreating the Jews. He blamed the Egyptian for unfair harassment. He probably even blamed the desert winds for blowing the sand off that stinkin' corpse, if that's how the murder was discovered.

But that's the problem. Blame is the primary reason it took forty years before Moses moved on! It wasn't God's inability to forgive. The problem wasn't God, it was MOSES! He was too busy playing the blame game!

A third way we deal with failure is we *shake it off.* While it's true that a failure constantly visited is a failure soon magnified, there's an equal danger in shaking it off too early.

In golf, when your drive barely makes it to the ladies' tees, it's extremely important that you shake it off. If you grouse about it for the next three holes, looking down the shaft of your $500 driver, convinced they sold you a lemon, you'll blow the whole round!

So it's true, you *do* need to shake off your failure! However—and this is so key: don't shake it off till you understand why you failed. That's what Moses didn't do. He shook it off too early.

Hell-bent on putting the mess behind him . . . get this: on the very same day Moses ran to Midian, he took a brand-new job, a job he'd grow to hate. And soon he got married!—to a woman with whom he likely struggled for the rest of his life (see Exodus 4:25, 18:2, 4-6.)

People, it takes time to learn from failure. So don't rush the process. Of course, there comes a time when you need to move on. But if you move on without reflecting on what you did and how you got here . . . if you fail to face up to the botched-up mess you've made of things? You'll just botch it up again!

However—and watch closely as I now talk out of the other side of my mouth—if you play that video too much? You could become so overwhelmed with guilt that you might just toss in the towel, call yourself a forever failure, and give up. That's what Moses did. He failed to learn what he needed to learn, so he couldn't move on when it was time to move on. And he wasted forty years of his life sitting by a well.

HOW NOT TO WALLOW

You know what Moses should have done? Four things. These four steps are action steps, not "sitting" steps—actions that can turn your "well" into a stepping-stone.

Accept Responsibility

Step #1 has to do with *responsibility*. As you sit by the well of your failure, whatever else you do—please! Accept the role you played. Don't play games. King David committed adultery, then arranged a murder to cover it up (2 Samuel 11:15). But when confronted with his sin? David came clean. He said, "I have sinned" (12:13). "I did it! It wasn't done to me; it was done *by* me!"

The hardest person to try to help is someone who conceals his weakness. When someone comes to see me, carrying himself as though life couldn't be better (though it's obvious his life is a wreck), there's not a thing I can say to help him. But if someone says, "Steve, I've really messed up," that's when we can really make tracks! That's when that failure, instead of a cumbersome weight dragging him down, can become wings that set him soaring again!

The first step to releasing your life into the grip of God's grace and getting up from that stupid well is to make an honest assessment of your responsibility in all of this. Not a soul-crushing, guilt-filled, depressing analysis that only prompts shame, but an open-hearted admission that says, "Apart from God, I'm a screw-up."

The Bible says, "If we confess our sins [*thereby admitting our responsibility in this circumstance*], he is faithful and just and will forgive . . . and purify us from all unrighteousness" (1 John 1:9).

So come clean. And do it now rather than later. I agree with former Vice President Alben Barkley. He said, "If you have to eat crow, at least eat it while it's hot."

Review It

Step #2 is *review.* Take the time to analyze why it happened. And don't you dare shake it off till you do.

Right now, in the middle of the mess, just say, "Lord, show me how I got here! Help me make sense of all this destruction. Teach me, Father, about myself. About why I do what I do and say what I say. Help me see me as clearly as You see me!"

Moses eventually learned the lessons he needed to learn. I'm convinced that he eventually prayed that kind of prayer. If he had prayed it sooner, he would have learned from his failure sooner, and those forty wasted years never would have happened.

What were the lessons Moses needed to learn?

First, he learned how to wait. He sat himself down, but in a decidedly different way this time. Instead of plopping down by some depressing well, Moses finally executed the Great Exchange. He stopped pressing his agenda and finally realized that although he was the right man trying to do the right job, it still wasn't the right time. So he waited.

He also learned about being a servant. After hanging out with smelly sheep, Moses learned that true leadership is more than grabbing the spotlight and barking out orders. A true leader is a servant (see Matthew 20:25-28).

But most of all, Moses learned that God didn't need his help.

Ernest Kurtz wrote a book he called *Not-God* because, he said, "That stands as the most important hurdle an addicted person can surmount: to acknowledge, deep in the soul, that he's not God. No mastery of manipulation and control, at which alcoholics excel, can overcome the root problem; rather, the alcoholic must recognize individual helplessness and fall back into the arms of the Higher Power. 'First of all, we had to quit playing God,' concluded the founders of AA; and then allow God himself to 'play God' in the addict's life, which involves daily, even moment-by-moment, surrender."[1]

Bill Wilson, cofounder of Alcoholics Anonymous, reached the unshakable conviction, now fundamental to twelve-step groups, that an alcoholic must hit bottom in order to climb out. Wilson said, "How privileged we are to understand so well the divine paradox that strength rises from weakness, that humiliation goes before resurrection: that pain is not only the price but the very touchstone of spiritual rebirth."[2]

So also is that true of failure.

Rehearse It

Which brings us to Step #3. Once you analyze why your failure happened and learn the lessons God wants you to learn, your next step is to *rehearse*. By that I mean, you need to *plan in advance* what you're going to do next time. It's not enough just to flag the error. To ensure you don't make that same mistake again, you've got to devise an alternative response plan so that next time, you're ready.

Before that ugly temptation returns for a second engagement
. . . before you're in a situation that prompts you to compromise . . . in advance—before that moment strikes—you've made
a mental decision regarding what you plan to do. And you've
rehearsed it in your mind over and over again.

Now if you don't do this? You'll keep making the same mistakes over and over again.

That's what stupid people do. You know, stupid people. Like
the farmer who asked the highway department to take down a
"Deer Crossing" sign. His reason? Too many deer were being hit,
and he didn't want them to cross there anymore.

Or stupid like the robber in a police lineup who, when asked to
repeat the phrase "Give me all your money or I'll shoot," exclaimed,
"That's not what I said!"

My favorite story about stupid people involves an Indiana
woman named Bonnie Booth. She was so annoyed by a painful
callus on her right big toe that she drank a gallon of vodka and
then grabbed the family shotgun and shot the callus right off her
foot! Later when asked why, she said she was afraid it was infected
because, and I quote, "It hurt real bad."

Now go ahead and laugh, but we all, sometimes, are stupid
people. We keep going to the same playgrounds and keep playing with the same playmates—and yet wonder why we keep having the same problems. Go figure. Listen, you've got to think it
through . . . ahead of time.

Lately, I've been living according to three axioms that can
help guide you as you review and rehearse:

1. If it ain't broke, don't fix it!
2. Once you know what works, do more of it!
3. If it doesn't work, don't do it again. Do something else![3]

Release It

Step #4 is *release.* Instead of erecting a monument to your failure and spending the rest of your life paying homage to it, you need to view your failure as a moment. Not a monument . . . a moment. A moment of instruction. A moment for correction. But just a moment. A moment from which you need to move on!

Our natural tendency is to so focus on our failure and so dwell on the disappointment that we get stuck in our setback.

But that's not what the Father wants for us. When we fail, He wants us to take responsibility. He also wants us to learn what we need to learn so it doesn't happen again. But then He wants us to move on! I don't believe for one second that God wanted Moses hanging around that well for forty years! That was Moses' problem!

Do you know what keeps many of us sitting at our well? Believing that God is impressed by our self-torture. That if we appear distraught enough or shamed enough, maybe He'll let us off the hook.

God doesn't want you beating yourself up . . . no matter what you've done. I know this because I know that when God looked down on mankind and saw a bunch of really messed-up people, He didn't get mad. He didn't dispatch some angelic SWAT team to wipe us from the face of the earth. Instead, He was so moved by our need, He sent His Son—not to discipline us, but to save us.

The Bible says that God "wants all [people] to be saved and to come to a knowledge of the truth" (1 Timothy 2:4). That's why He freely offers mercy.

GOD, YOU'RE FIRED!

In his book *A Hunger for Healing,* J. Keith Miller tells of a man who joined a twelve-step group. As he talked with one of the veterans, he said, "No way am I going to turn my life over to God. He'd ruin me, and I'd deserve it."

This guy saw God, not as a God of mercy, but as a cosmic policeman. And his experiences with the police weren't very positive. You know what the old-timer said?

"Son, you ought to fire your god. You've got the wrong god for this program. The God who operates here is loving, forgiving and gives you all the chances you need to get with the program. I used to have a god like yours—when I first came. But I had to fire him, and I got me a new God!"[4]

Some of you need to fire your god, too. Now save your cards and letters; I know there is only one God. It's just that the god many perceive God to be is not the true God at all! And we need to fire that misconception and discover all over again the true God of the Bible.

You need to fire that god whose only emotions are anger and disappointment and frustration toward all your many failures. You need to fire that god who says he loves you but is never there for you, that god who always tells you what you ought to do but never tells you how to do it. That god who says, "I knew you'd blow it" . . . you need to give that god his walking papers.

Instead, you need to surrender to a new God. A God who, in fact, is not new at all. He's the God of the Bible; it's just that some folks have skewed the truth of who He really is. He's the God who described himself as full of mercy and rich in grace (see James 5:11 and Ephesians 2:7). A God who's there to pick you up when you fall, who's dependable and honest, who cares enough to confront you but loves you way too much ever to condemn you.

And until you turn to *that* God, you're going to keep sitting by the well—nursing your wounds and cursing your past. You'll think, *There's no grace for someone like me. I blew it. No more chances. My life, as I know it, is over.*

No! Listen, God loves you. And He knows what you've been through. He left Heaven so you could go to Heaven. He went through hell so you wouldn't have to.

And just before He died, He said, "It is finished" (John 19:30). You know what that means? It means, "I completed the job I was given. The Father sent me to be your deliverer, and I did it! It's done. Failure has been defeated! So stop wallowing in guilt. Stop trying to paper over your sin. And please! Stop sitting by the well. I want you to experience my grace because no matter what you've done, I love you. And I will forgive you. So come on, let's start over."

Now maybe you're not ready to go there. Neither was Moses. That's why he sat by that well. And not a day passed when he didn't wish for a mulligan! "But God could never use me. Not after what I've done."

Oh, really?

In Exodus 3, we resume Moses' story. It was a day much like any other day. Moses was herding his father-in-law's sheep to a new spot so they could graze, a spot where the only sounds Moses could hear were the bleating of sheep and the lonely whine of his broken heart.

When all of a sudden, a bush caught fire! Not an altogether unheard-of experience in the desert—but for some reason, on this day, unlike other days, Moses said, "I will go over and see this strange sight—why the bush does not burn up" (Exodus 3:3).

Personally, I can't help but wonder if God had torched a lot of other bushes, too, but Moses was too guilt-ridden to see them.

But this time he looked.

And "when the LORD saw that he had gone over to look, God called to him from within the bush" (v. 4).

What was God's message? "Go, Moses. It's time—in fact, it's way past time for you to fulfill your calling. Stop whining and move out! God said, "I am sending you to Pharaoh to bring my people . . . out of Egypt" (v. 10).

And don't you know how that "you" must have reverberated in Moses' heart? Like the sound of the crowd at a ball game when an opposing player is called for a crucial foul: "You, you, you!"

What did Moses say? Well, what does any "failure" say? "Who am I, that I should go to Pharaoh?" (v. 11).

That's a far cry from Moses' earlier boasts. Moses had learned some valuable lessons during those "sitting years." Maybe some of those lessons he learned *too* well.

Maybe that's why he deferred God's call not once, but six times. Each time God said, "Go," Moses answered, "No." Years before, he leaped at the chance to help his people. Now . . . well, Moses isn't so sure anymore.

The Lord finally says to Moses, "What is that in your hand?"

"A staff" (4:2).

LOSING THE CRUTCH

Now the truth is, it was more than just a staff. That hunk of wood was a poignant reminder of Moses' past. It was the tool of a new trade forced on him because of his sin. A symbol of his impatient, prideful spirit, which had charged ahead of God and demanded his own way. So in a very real sense that staff had become Moses' crutch.

And every time Moses even thought about going to Egypt, he'd lean on that staff—and remember every wretched detail of his past—and conclude that God could never use someone like him. But God said to Moses, "Throw it on the ground" (v. 3). I think He meant, "Come on, release it, dude! Put this behind you! Release your past, Moses, and just watch what I can do with it!"

So Moses did. And God got himself a deliverer, while Moses . . . got that mulligan.

People, that bush was not just for Moses. It's a sign to you and me as well. It's a powerful reminder that God loves to use failures, no matter how scarred by sin.

The fact is God can use you, and He wants to. In fact, chances are good He's waiting for you, just as He waited for Moses, to get over what you've done and look at what God alone can do.

I'm convinced there are burning bushes all around your life right now. God has strategically placed little pockets of grace within your view as He seeks to provide forgiveness, but you won't see them. With blinders firmly in place, you stubbornly sit by the well, staring at the ground, heaving sighs as big as Texas.

You've given up. When what you really need to do to move from whining to winning is say, "Lord, I'm not much. I've failed miserably. But if You can use a failure like Moses, maybe You can use me, too. So here I am."

And you know what? He'll do it. He'll redeem your dream! Because He doesn't want you to give up! And dying for your sin? It's already been done. For you to live for Jesus in spite of sin— that's what charges God's batteries!

So come on. Join the ranks of other "failures" God has used. Failures like Noah the Drunkard, David the Adulterer, Solomon the Compromiser. How about Abraham the Liar, Samson the Womanizer, Thomas the Doubter, Zacchaeus the Crook, Peter the Denier and even Paul the Persecutor!

These and hundreds like them were all used by God . . . despite their score cards. That they blew it is obvious. But they accepted God's grace, and in that grace they moved on.

Think it's time for you to move on, too? To push away from the well, answer the call of the bush, and move on?

I know you feel guilty. You feel wrong, washed up, and totally undeserving. But that's a good thing because that means you're right at the place of God's greatest use of your life. And God, in grace, is shouting, "Come on, dude! Get up off that stone by that well! We've got a dream to do!"

But as you get up? Make sure you throw that ugly, confining staff down! OK? Just let it go!

THROW IT DOWN

For Moses, that staff was a constant reminder that he had blown it. No wonder God told him to throw it down! And the staff you carry? That dark, ever-present reminder of your past sin? It's more than a staff, isn't it? It's a crutch—a crutch that has, for far too long, haunted you and sidelined you.

So every time you see God's bush—and even think about giving yourself to some new calling—that staff blocks your way. It shouts to your heart whatever label you've allowed someone to give you: Liar! Divorcee! Adulterer! Former mental patient! Listen, you've got to throw that thing down.

Ken Medema's anthem "Moses" looks at Moses' staff as a symbol of failure, a daily reminder of past sin, like a scar or disfigurement . . . a scarlet letter. A security blanket, too—Moses' excuse for never trying again.

But at the end, Moses is standing at the bush, clutching his crutch, adamantly shaking his head no, and God says, "Moses . . ."

> "What do you hold in your hand today?
> To what or to whom are you bound?
> Are you willing to give it to God right now?
> Give it up. Let it go. Throw it down."

That's God's message. I don't know what you've done. I don't know the past that keeps weighing you down. But what I *do* know is this: it's time. It's time to throw it down, to bury your past at the foot of the cross, and let God use you again.

So come on. Give it up. Let it go. Throw it down.

CHAPTER 7

TRADING SHEEP FOR SUBJECTS

I'VE GOT A CONFESSION to make: I really enjoy movies. Ask my wife, Cindy. In those rare moments when we've got a little time—and nothing vital we have to do with that time—my first inclination (much to her dismay) is, "Let's go to a movie!"

After drawing a deep breath and then slowly exhaling, she'll try to sound perky. "OK . . . whatcha wanna see?"

To which I typically reply, "I don't care!"

See, I'm very undiscerning when it comes to movies. I'll watch just about anything! For example, I paid perfectly good money and invested ninety-two minutes watching *Napoleon Dynamite*. I don't know why. I think I've got a problem! I even saw *Dude, Where's My Car?* Somebody, please help me!

If you're not familiar with those films, it's probably just as well. They're not exactly Oscar contenders.

To complete my confession—and this revealing behind-the-scenes look at my utter lack of good taste—you should probably also know that my favorite comedy film of all time is *Blazing Saddles*!

So it's true—I have almost no taste when it comes to watching flicks.

And the reason is clear: movies are a diversion for me. When I go to a movie, I'm not looking so much to be entertained as to find an escape!

It's really kind of cool to sit in a dark room, shift into neutral, munch on some popcorn, hold hands with my lady, and watch as other people struggle with thorny issues, issues that (unlike my own) magically get resolved in about an hour and a half!

Which, right there, ought to tell you something: movies aren't real, people. Let me repeat that for you hardcore users: movies aren't real. Life simply does not and cannot work out like it happens on the silver screen.

By the way, I came across a list of things that happen only in the movies. Are you ready? In the movies:

All telephone numbers begin with 555.

Dinosaurs eat only the ugly people.

All computer disks will work in all computers, regardless of software.

If a killer is lurking in your house, it's easy to find him. Just run some bath water, and while the room is steaming up, look in the mirror and there he'll be!

Creepy music coming from a cemetery must always be investigated.

The person you trust most is probably trying to kill you.

The more a man and a woman hate each other, the more likely it is they will fall in love.

If you fall in love, it's customary to burst into song—especially if you're walking down a crowded street.

And if you decide to start dancing down the street, lo and behold, everyone else on the block will instantly know all the steps.

That's just the way life works . . . in the movies.

One reason I've been thinking about movies is because I'm writing this chapter on Oscar night. You know, that one night each

year when people who already get more attention than they need—and more accolades than they deserve—get even more!

Oscar night is so surreal that the honorees can't even walk on perfectly clean sidewalks; we've got to line them with red carpet! And it's not enough simply to broadcast the show anymore; we've got to have preshows just so we can find out, "Who are you wearing?"

And even though many people never see most of the movies nominated, and even though we often love every movie the critics hate . . . over a billion people tune in to watch the Oscars.

Why? Because I'm not the only one who loves the movies! Even though great movies don't necessarily reflect real life, or maybe *because* they don't, we love the movies.

While listening to all the pre-Oscar hype, it occurred to me that the real-life story of King David is the stuff great movies are made of. The main plot alone is enough to keep our interest: a lowly shepherd boy trades his staff for a scepter, his sheep for subjects, his favorite tree stump for a throne.

And talk about a multidimensional leading role! Forget Michael Keaton in *Multiplicity* or Eddie Murphy in *The Klumps*. What about David playing the roles of shepherd, hunter, giant-killer, musician, warrior, hero, poet, outlaw, ladies man, warlord, composer, prophet, worship leader, murderer, builder, leader, husband, son, parent . . . and, of course, king!

DAVID: THE MOVIE

But what makes David's projected movie a shoo-in blockbuster is the subtext of his story. The big story, of course, is that a shepherd boy became a king. But the story behind the story has more twists than a bag of pretzels and more unexpected turns than a hamster maze! Seriously! If I were to write a screenplay about David, words like *unexpected* and *surprising* and even *out of the blue* would be in great abundance. Folks, we're talking more twists than Chubby Checker on speed!

The pick of the litter. If this were a movie, David's older brother Eliab would have easily been the one cast in the title role. Instead, the runt became the pick of the litter.

God had chosen one of Jesse's sons to be Israel's new king (see 1 Samuel 16:1). So when Samuel caught a glimpse of Eliab, he thought, "Surely the LORD's anointed stands here before the LORD" (v. 6). Why'd he have such an immediate reaction? For one thing, Eliab was the eldest of Jesse's eight sons. For another, Eliab was one striking specimen! He was easy on the eyes . . . solid as a rock . . . and most important, as tall as a mountain. I'm guessing that because Saul, Israel's first king, was tall, too (1 Samuel 9:2; 10:23). And there's nothing like tall to make someone look king-like, right? So Eliab looked the part. He looked like Saul.

But wait. The whole reason Samuel was anointing a new king was because Saul was such a lousy king! He may have looked the part, but he didn't have the right heart! That's why God rejected him! So although Eliab had quite the impressive outward appearance, the big question was, what was he like on the inside?

And that's why the Lord serves notice that when He casts a part, it's all about heart! "Do not consider his appearance or his height, for I have rejected him. The LORD does not look at the things man looks at. Man looks at the outward appearance, but the LORD looks at the heart" (16:7).

That's when the parade of candidates began. First came Abinadab, but Samuel said, "He's not the one." Then Shammah. "Not him either." All told, verse 10 says, "Jesse had seven of his sons pass before Samuel."

Can you imagine? Waiting in the wings, prepping for the audition of a lifetime. It doesn't get any better than being king! So they're combing their hair, doing their nails, and picking their teeth because they realize that with each succeeding rejection, *I might just be the one!*

But Samuel said, "The LORD has not chosen these" (v. 10). Then he asked a very revealing question: "Are these all the sons you have?" (v. 11). Meaning, "Sorry for asking, but God clearly told me He'd chosen one of your kiddos. Surely these aren't your only boys."

Did it leave a scar? First Samuel 16:11 tells us, "'There is still the youngest,' Jesse said, 'but he is tending the sheep.'" I can almost hear Jesse thinking, *Come to think of it—I DO have another kid, don't I?* Wow! Poor David wasn't even on Jesse's radar! David's dad had rejected—or at the very least, neglected—him.

Did his dad's neglect leave a scar?

A mom asked me that once. Recognizing that her son's father had never given him what he needed, she wanted to know, "Will it leave a scar?"

You know what I told her? "I'm sorry but, yeah, there will be a scar. But not necessarily a deforming scar or even a defacing scar. This experience could be your son's defining scar."

Such was the case for David. He was a nobody—even in the eyes of his own dad. (But if you want to know why David ruled Israel with such a gentle sensitivity, there's your clue. And I think David used that defining experience as motivation to try to be a better father than his dad.)

I heard a leader once say that he routinely asks likely hirees about their relationship with their fathers. And if that relationship wasn't good he won't hire the person. Because he believes if you don't have a solid relationship with your dad, you will not be a good leader.

There's a Greek word for that kind of thinking: *baloney!* Really! Based on that flawed and horizontally focused requirement, the dude would have passed on David! Can you imagine?

OK, maybe David didn't look the part. But don't you get it? God doesn't see us the way we see ourselves. God sees us—every single one of us—not for what we are, but for what, through Him, we can be.

Jesse didn't even honor David as one of his sons. And to his brothers, he was a scruffy, smelly shepherd boy. But to God? David was a king!

Samuel knew it the instant he laid eyes on the kid. The Lord confirmed it, saying, "Rise and anoint him; he is the one" (v. 12). And in a twist rivaling those found in Allen Iverson's hair, the runt was now the pick of the litter. Jesse's forgotten shepherd boy had oil running down his neck—and everybody talking about a crown and a throne and baby brother as king!?

He didn't look the part. Why did God choose David? Because even though he didn't look the part, David had the right heart. He was a man, as Samuel described him, "after [God's] own heart" (13:14).

Second Chronicles 16:9 says that "the eyes of the LORD range throughout the earth to strengthen those whose hearts are fully committed to him." And the Lord found in David just such a heart. Fully devoted, wholly surrendered, utterly committed. David loved the things that God loves. What was important to the Lord was important to him. And that's why God chose him.

Talk about the complete package! Listen to Psalm 78:70-72: "[The Lord] chose David his servant and took him from the sheep pens; from tending the sheep he brought him to be the shepherd of his people Jacob, of Israel his inheritance. And David shepherded them with integrity of heart; with skillful hands he led them."

Please note that order. He shepherded with integrity first and then with skill. Interesting. Our culture thinks skill is all that matters in leadership.

We don't care what our leaders do behind closed doors. I don't want to know what he does when nobody's looking. All I care about is, "Is he doing the job?"

And it's true, David had mad skill! He was a tough, courageous warrior, a thoughtful and sensitive musician, a seasoned outdoorsman, a leader of men, and a powerful public speaker.

But what good is skill if your leader lies to you? Or talent if he promotes only his own agenda? What good is ability if you're never sure when he's telling you the truth?

David was a man of skill, yes. But even more, a man of integrity. When he tended sheep (a job so degrading no one ever bothered to investigate), he did the job right. If a lamb wandered away, he didn't say, "No one will know." He'd find that lamb and bring her home. And when he shepherded Israel? He cared for his people the same way.

One of the ways you can see David's integrity is in what he did immediately after Samuel anointed him.

Did he go to the palace and say, "Hey Saul, scoot over. It's my turn"? No.

Did he scurry over to Party City and start trying on crowns? No.

Did he go to the copy shop and make business cards announcing "King-elect"? No!

You know what David did? With the oil still dripping down his back, he went back to the sheep.

Later, when Saul hired him to play music, every movie buff will agree that was David's big break! The genesis of his meteoric rise to power! Pack your bags for the big time, David! Instead, he packed his gear every night and went right back to the sheep.

And even when he downed Goliath and the crowds enthusiastically sang his praise—even then . . . right back to the sheep.

From the perspective of a seasoned moviegoer, how twisted is that? More twists than a case of Twizzlers, I'd say! But God called it integrity. For thirteen years David herded and waited . . . with integrity.

His new crib was a cave. Now stay tuned, because although David's life sounds like a fairy tale—what with a prophet pouring oil down his neck and a cushy gig singing in the palace lounge and a fanciful battle involving a giant and a leather slingshot, not to mention all those adoring fans cheering him at the gates—the fact is, David didn't exactly waltz to Israel's throne. No, instead of packing for the palace, David's new crib would be a cave.

I told you his story had more twists than a garden hose. And do you know why David's life got worse before it got better? Because of all those fans singing at the gates.

Because somebody else heard those songs, too. And although he was glad Goliath was gone, King Saul couldn't bear the thought that somebody else would get credit for it. 1 Samuel 18:9 says, "From that time on Saul kept a jealous eye on David."

That doesn't even begin to describe it.

MORE TWISTS AND TURNS

You want to talk about plot twists? The next chapter of David's life has more twists than a dime-store novel. More twists than a French braid. More twists than my small intestines. (And with that I will stop.)

He lost his job. Twist #1 came when David lost his job. Yeah, the music gig! He was hired to play music whenever Saul had one of his infamous mood swings. And even though David knew that Saul hated his guts, he played anyway! One day while David was singing a James Taylor ballad, Saul actually grabbed a spear and chucked it right at the guy! David probably thought, *Note to self: don't ever play "Fire and Rain" again!*

Meanwhile, everybody else was thinking, *Saul! Cut back on the caffeine, dawg!*

That's Saul. There was no good reason for such a nasty display. Yet Saul heaved another spear at him, and when David ducked this time, he heard the whooshing sound as it screamed by his skull—and then, *thud!* buried itself in the wall. And while the spear was still going *booiiinnngg*, David ran for his life. That led to Twist #2:

He lost his wife. David had married Saul's daughter Michal. But then one day Saul sent soldiers to David's house to kill him; and when Michal helped David escape, Saul took her captive. And then forced her to marry somebody else.

He lost his mentor. The spiral continues with Twist #3 as David roamed the countryside trying to find some refuge, till finally, he found Samuel. Makes sense. Samuel's the one who had anointed him and had served for years as David's spiritual mentor. Surely David would be safe there.

Yet when Saul heard where David was hiding, "he sent men to capture him" (19:20). Which meant David had to skedaddle. And since Samuel was too old to skedaddle, David skedaddled alone.

For those keeping track, David has now lost his job, his family, and his trusted mentor.

He lost his best friend. What was still left to lose? How about his best friend? Even though Jonathan was King Saul's son and David was King Saul's arch-nemesis, Jonathan and David were great friends. So close were these two that when Jonathan defended David, Saul chucked a spear at him, too! Yet even then, their love remained strong. There was just one problem—Saul wasn't backin' down, and Jonathan couldn't cross him. So after a tearful farewell, David headed for the wilderness—without a job, a wife, a mentor . . . and now, without a friend. Twist #4.

Talk about Putting Off and Putting On! Except in this season of David's life, *off* was the only obvious adverb. What God was putting *on* that man wasn't known . . . even to David. I mean, here's a man who had decided to do life God's way, not his own. This hard-charging leader type had willingly relinquished his timetable for God's. And having made the Great Exchange, David waited. And waited some more.

But doggone it, all this "losing" along the way? Well, it was starting to get a little old.

And that's when the twist-ee in this story became twist-ed. That's when David ran amuck. God had taken some things away from David that David greatly valued. But then David got into the act, and he gave away even more.

His First Gaffe Was Gath

His first stopover was a place called Gath. Anybody remember hearing that name before? "Yeah, the big guy . . . Goliath . . . that's where he came from! Are you tellin' me David wandered into the camp of the enemy?" That's exactly what I'm telling you.

This seems to be the first time David didn't pray about what he should do—he just did it! David isn't inquiring of the Lord—he's not praying, he's not writing psalms, and he's not singing worship tunes, either. Truth is, David is panicked! So he packs his bags . . . for Gath?

Trouble is, the people of Gath remembered David—and not so fondly. So David, fearing for his life, pretended to be insane. "He acted like a madman, making marks on the doors of the gate and letting saliva run down his beard" (21:13). Do you see the irony in that? The same man who once had oil running down his neck now had slobber running down his beard!?

Which is why, when the coast was clear, "David left Gath and escaped to the cave of Adullam" (22:1). He was supposed to be living in a palace by now. Instead, he was crouching in a cave. With no money, no friends, no job—David was running for his life with no hope that life was ever gonna get any better.

Maybe you're in a cave, too. Maybe you've lost your job. Or maybe you're under severe financial pressure. Maybe your dreams for a family have been shattered.

Whatever has happened, you're in a cave. And it's so very easy in that cave to wonder, *Does God even know where I am? Has He forgotten His promise?*

May I speak to you as one cave dweller to another? Having spent time in my own cave, I've learned a lot about caves. For one, I've learned that caves are where God does His best work. Quite unlike most other places on earth, a cave makes a good place for God to mold and shape His children.

Because sometimes you've got to have all your props and crutches and security blankets stripped away so that all you have left is God. And that's when you realize: God is enough. He really is!

And all those props you thought were supporting you? They're nothing more than popcorn and Jujubes.

Now we'd like to think we could learn such lessons in the palace—but we can't. God does this kind of work in caves.

We don't have a definite chronology, but as best we can tell, David spent ten years crouching in caves. And I'm convinced he was convinced that God would never make good on His promise.

A Burg Called Ziklag

That's why he tried another goodwill gesture to the King of Philistia. And this time the king took him up on it. He gave David his own town, a burg called Ziklag. And David and his family, plus his militia and their families, came to live in Ziklag.

The only problem with this arrangement was that God wasn't in it. And He wasn't in it because God knows if you associate with Philistines, in time you'll start acting like Philistines. Live in the camp of the enemy long enough, and in time you will adopt your enemy's mind-set. That's why the Bible says, "Bad company corrupts good character" (1 Corinthians 15:33).

I like what Chuck Swindoll says about that: "If you put on white gloves and start working in the mud, the gloves always get muddy; never does the mud get glovey."

And sure enough, Ziklag didn't get glovey; David got muddy. Separated from those who knew him, with no reputation to live up to, no structure to shape or define him, David began compromising in ways he never would have imagined.

Even worse, David lost contact with God. For three chapters in the Bible, a time period covering nearly eighteen months, there's nothing happening between David and God! Nothing!

Now though he lost his spiritual edge, there's one thing David didn't lose: his thirst for battle. This guy really liked killin' people! So when the Philistines decided to do battle against Israel? David, man of war that he was, brought his militia to Philistine Enlistment Day and signed up to fight against his own people!

But the Philistines didn't trust David that much! They'd heard those Israeli fight songs that were like the McDonald's sign, boasting billions and billions served—except David's fans used to sing, "Saul has slain his thousands, and David his tens of thousands" (1 Samuel 18:7). And the Philistines weren't all that keen about being the reason for updating David's résumé!

So David and his men headed back home to Ziklag.

The story is recorded in 1 Samuel 30, and we're told there that as David's men topped the last hill leading into Ziklag, eager to see their wives and children, they were greeted instead by charred ruins and billowing clouds of thick, black smoke. They raced into the city, anxiously shouting the names of their loved ones—frantically digging through the rubble—and discovered, to their grief, that every wife, son, daughter, cow, and lamb was gone. Some invading marauders had raided the city; the city was burned and their families were gone!

The Bible says these battle-hardened tough guys were so brokenhearted, they "wept aloud [*get this*] until they had no strength left to weep" (30:4).

Have you ever wept like that? Have you ever cried so much you didn't have any tears left? That's the grief in this moment. "My wife is missing!" "What have they done to my daughter?" They're devastated!

So devastated that these same men who'd once come crawling to David "in distress or in debt or discontented" (22:2) now suddenly turned on their leader! These were the same men who had found in David a relief from hard times. David had skillfully reshaped them from a sorry tribe of losers and lowlifes into a lean, mean, Philistine-fighting machine. These same men had learned to love each other and had been the first line of defense for each other.

You understand how that happens. Hurting people hurt people, right? You go through a loss, endure some kind of heartache, and what happens? You invariably try to find somebody, anybody, to blame. And David was an easy target.

After all, he's the one who brought them to this dive in the first place—then left the town totally unprotected because he wanted to go play war against his own people!

So with hearts bent on mutiny, these men David had trained into an army of valiant warriors turned on him!

David's family was gone, too—but that didn't matter to these guys! Their hearts were broken; so they lashed out, and David was forced to absorb every angry blow.

Now let that sink in. David lost yet another family, his friends, and his entire support system.

How did he respond *this* time?

WHAT DAVID GOT RIGHT

Till now, God had been demoted to the sidelines. With every passing month, David slipped further and further down the drain. Deeper and deeper into an abyss of despair, darkness, and defeat. Why? Because David was manning the controls. God never led David to Philistia. That was David's stupid scheme!

But now, for the first time in a long time, David looks not to his own devices but to the Lord.

Strength in the Lord

Realizing his life had spiraled out of control when *he* was in charge, David refuses to dig into his trusty little bag o' tricks and pull out yet another harebrained scheme! Not this time! No, this time David seeks the Lord and reestablishes his faith connection. For a while he's done Putting Off, and the first thing he Puts On, 1 Samuel 30:6 tells us, results in finding his strength in the Lord.

And folks, that's always the first step back home. Faith is always the beginning of the beginning of a changed life.

When you're living in the land of compromise and wandering in a place far removed from God, you're out of touch. And before long, you're out of control. And if you don't get with it? You'll soon be out of hope.

As with so many of us, it took the collapse of David's outer world before his inner heart was ready to seek God again.

Yet, in the moment he began? For the first time in a long time, David was strengthened . . . again. Listen, it doesn't matter how low you go—or who rejects you or slanders you or turns his back on you—God, in the moment you look to Him for strength, will give it freely.

Sometime later, David wrote a song, Psalm 138, about this moment: "In the moment I called out, you stepped in; you made my life large with strength" (v. 3, THE MESSAGE). "Though I walk in the midst of trouble, you preserve my life" (v. 7, NIV).

Look carefully at those words. Based on David's testimony, how do you find strength in the Lord? You call out, right? That's what you do. You tell God, in whatever feeble words trickle out, that you need Him! That you can't take another step, you can't live another day, you can't draw another breath unless He is with you. That's what David did.

A Beeline for Abiathar

But that's not all he did. Having reestablished his connection with God, David took a second step. He made a beeline for Abiathar the priest. He went, essentially, to his pastor in search of godly counsel.

And that's a big deal, folks. Samuel had always been David's mentor, but David hadn't been listening to Samuel for a long time. . . almost as long as David's life had been tubing out!

And you want to talk out of control? During David's rebellion, he lied to a priest, stole holy bread from the temple, scratched graffiti on city property, and slobbered in public like the village idiot. All because he refused to submit to godly counsel!

But now, everything has changed. Realizing his desperate condition, David named his need before God, and then he did what *we* need to do; he went to a trusted adviser. David said, "Bring me the ephod." Now the ephod was a priestly robe with a special pocket, and in this pocket were the Urim and the Thummim—two gems or stones. Whenever the priest wanted to know God's will, he'd shake those rocks around, reach in, and then the stone he pulled out gave the Lord's yes or no. Wouldn't it be great if we still had ephods today?

Abiathar brought the ephod, and David asked his question. "Should I pursue those who did this? And if I do, will I catch 'em?"

I can see Abiathar reach in, shake the rocks, mumble some-thing about "seven come eleven," then pull one out. Which one do you think he selected? It was Thummim, baby! God said, "David, move out already!"

So David and his men bugged out like school kids at recess!

And it was in the midst of doing battle against his adversaries that David discovered a truth about God that would serve him well for the rest of his life.

David discovered that God is more than a creator. More than a defender. More than a rock, a strong tower, or a mighty shield. David discovered that our God loves to recover what we think is gone forever. That our God has a knack for taking back whatever has been taken away.

You see, the recovery on this day was absolute. Not one wife, not one child was lost. Nothing that had been taken was still missing.

NOTHING MISSING

In fact, listen to how Scripture describes this victory: "David fought them from dusk until the evening of the next day. . . . David recovered everything the Amalekites had taken. . . . Nothing was missing: young or old, boy or girl, plunder or anything else they had taken. David brought everything back" (1 Samuel 30:17-19).

Even more incredible than that was the other "stolen property" God recovered. Because a mere fifty-four verses after that verse—it's hard to believe—"The men of Judah came to Hebron and there they anointed David king" (2 Samuel 2:4).

You movie fans are thinking, *Well, that's cool, but that's it?*

That's it.

You mean, after thirteen years dodging spears and crouching in caves, that's all the fanfare David gets? Come on, this is an epic moment! God's promise . . . finally fulfilled! Israel's greatest king ascends to the throne!

So where are the shofar trumpets? And the dancers and the food and crowds shouting in frenzy as David is carried to his place of honor, anointed with oil and fitted with a crown?

Where is Mel Gibson when you need him?

But see, that's the problem—this isn't the movies. This is real life!

So David had a coronation befitting a sheepherding, bear-wrestling, giant-killing cave dweller who'd zigzagged his way from the wilderness to the caves to Ziklag—and finally, to the palace.

But hang in there! Just because he's been crowned doesn't mean the movie's over. I know that's how it works in Hollywood. Hollywood is all about milking the climax, right? So in Hollywood, the climax in David's story is his coronation! And all those barriers—those twists and turns along the way? They just kept things interesting!

But remove the barriers—get David out of the caves and into the palace—and let's strike up the band and cue the singers. Turn on the bubble machine! Let's have a party!

Because once the oil is applied and the crown is fixed in place, the movie's over.

Fade to black.

Roll the credits.

The end.

However, if that's how you feel, you've missed the point. This isn't the movies. And David's story isn't over just because he finally reached the throne.

No, the real climax of this story—and the hint that God had been planning a sequel all along—is that the first thing this new king does . . . is the same thing he did at Ziklag. Which was also the same thing he did before he fought Goliath. Which was also the same thing he did, as a teen, as he walked among the woollies.

Do you see it? "David inquired of the Lord" (2:1). No party, no coronation ball—just a humble shepherd-boy-turned-king, finding his strength and his counsel in the Lord. Which is exactly what God needed to teach him—and why those twists and turns along the way had to happen.

David did the same thing in chapter 5 when he was made king over all of Israel. Once again David "inquired of the Lord" (vv. 19, 23). And having inquired, verse 25 says, "David did as the Lord commanded." He was king, yet from day one David freely submitted to the King of kings.

No wonder he became "more and more powerful, because the Lord God Almighty was with him" (v. 10).

Nobody ever said Trading Places was easy. But what was true for David is equally true for you: every twist and every turn in your story—as you live a life fully renovated and well lived before God—is preparing you, too, for an epic so all-encompassing, so amazing, that no silver screen could *ever* contain it.

CHAPTER 8

TRADING BEAUTY FOR BRAVERY

NEW ORLEANS WAS IN TURMOIL. A federal judge had ordered the city to open its public schools to black children. The white parents decided if they had to let black children in, they'd just keep their children out. What's more, they made it known that any black child who came to school would pay a price. So the black children stayed home, too.

Except Ruby Bridges. She wanted to go to school, so her parents sent her—all by herself, all of six years old. She was the first, and for a while the only, black child to attend class in a white New Orleans public school.

Every morning she walked all alone through a heckling crowd. Angry white people lined up on along the street and shook fists at her, threatening to do harm to her if she kept coming to their school. Yet every morning at ten minutes before eight, Ruby walked—head up and shoulders back—right through the belly of that hateful mob. Then she spent the entire day alone inside that silent school building.

Professor Robert Coles wanted to know what made Ruby so courageous, so he talked to her mama. Here's what Ruby's mama had to say: "There's a lot of people who talk about doing good, and a lot of people who argue about what'd be good and what'd not be good, but there are other folks who just put their lives on the line for what's right."[1]

True, but there aren't a lot of "other folks" willing to do that. Thankfully, there are a few. They are forever enshrined in our hearts, so enamored are we by their courageous deeds.

Mother Teresa, for example. She was the featured speaker at the 1994 National Prayer Breakfast. When she took the podium, that ninety-pound powerhouse passionately pleaded for the lives of unborn children. She could barely be seen over the lectern, and with her stooped back and gnarled, arthritic fingers she was hardly a symbol of anything even resembling power. Yet she stood before those dignitaries and said, "The greatest destroyer of peace today is abortion . . . [for] if we accept that a mother can kill even her own child, how can we tell other people not to kill each other?" She said, "Please, don't kill the child! I want the child. Please give me the child."[2]

And what about Abraham Lincoln, who abolished slavery on January 1, 1863, with the Emancipation Proclamation's declaration that "all persons held as slaves . . . are, and henceforward shall be free."

Or Anne Sullivan, who bravely taught the "uneducable" Helen Keller?

Or Martin Luther King, who dreamed a dream "that my four children will one day live in a nation where they will not be judged by the color of their skin but by the content of their character."[3]

Or Ronald Reagan, standing alongside the Berlin Wall—that symbol of hate and untold destruction—and stubbornly insisting, "Mr. Gorbachev, tear down this wall!"

There are other names. Thomas Edison, who refused to quit even when all others did, and because he persevered, we have light over our shoulders today. Douglas MacArthur, who, in the darkest days of World War II, said, "I shall return." And he did! Martin Luther, standing before the emperor of the Roman Empire. Ordered to recant his alleged heresy against the church, Luther refused, saying, "Here I stand, God help me; I can do no other."

And what about other equally brave souls for whom we have no name?

That courageous student in Tiananmen Square who stared down an entire tank column, capturing the imagination of the world and defining a nation's struggle to embrace freedom.

Or the Christian evangelist in the African country of Chad, who, because of his faith in Jesus, was sewn inside a drum and slowly starved to death while drummers feverishly pounded those skins.

Or in Indonesia, where a fifteen-year-old boy, though threatened by a mob, refused to renounce Christ. An attacker swung a sword at him, missed, and ripped his Bible. The next swing sliced open the boy's abdomen, and his body was mercilessly thrown into a ditch. His final words? "I am a soldier for Christ!"[4]

And what about biblical heroes like Noah, who built a boat in the desert and saved the human race? Or Moses, who took on Pharaoh and freed Israel from bondage. Or Joseph, tossed in a pit, then prison—yet he emerged from both to feed a starving nation and save his people from extinction.

I've studied these valiant change agents—these determined difference makers—and I've found that this noble tribe shares four rare and exceedingly precious attributes:

Each made a costly, personal commitment to his cause.

Each also took overt and risky action.

Each obviously made an unquestioned impact.

Each also was—don't miss this—just one person.

Not an army of many but just one solitary soldier. One man, one woman, one little girl who refused to walk away. Alone, yet armed with a vision of what life could be—or should be—or *must* be—they moved out!

Some were persons of influence, that's true. Most were regular Joes . . . hardy souls who had a purpose and a passion that refused to be denied. They were armed with that purpose and passion—and hardly more than that—by a factor best described as the power of one, and they literally changed their world!

THE POWER OF ONE

May I add another name to that list? It's not a name you might readily recall. Primarily because it belongs to an orphaned Jewish girl raised in Persia by a relative. Not exactly fodder for greatness.

Yet I agree with Mary Tyler Moore: "You can't be brave if you've only had wonderful things happen to you."[5] That's so true. And talk about going through stuff? Esther had lived life in the raw. Raised in a country where people of "her kind" were wildly hated. Raised, not by her parents, but by a male cousin. Yet somehow Esther tapped into a hidden strength that even she didn't know she had.

Her story is told in the Old Testament book that bears her name. And it's an unusual Bible book for a couple reasons:

For one, the name of God is never even mentioned. However, commentator Matthew Henry got it right when he said, "The name of God is not here, but His finger is." God's actions are clearly in play. His presence dominates the story line. His plan is clearly the prevailing theme. But His name never appears. Max Lucado suggests: "Could it be that God is more concerned about getting the job done than getting credit?"[6]

Another unique thing about this book is it's one of only two Bible books named after a woman. And in this case, a very strong-minded, independent woman, who emerges from virtual obscurity to save her nation from extinction.

Now when I say obscurity, I mean *obscurity.* Esther had been orphaned at an early age. She was adopted by her cousin Mordecai during the time Israel was languishing in Babylonian captivity. Mordecai took on the role of a beloved uncle to Esther. He faithfully taught Esther the ways of her nation Israel, and he also taught her to love Israel's God.

As Esther grew up, she became a beautiful young woman. I'm not being sexist when I say that her beauty is a huge part of the story.

History tells us that King Xerxes had just returned from war, and his army had been soundly defeated. In addition, his marriage to Queen Vashti had ended in disaster (Esther 1:19-21). So his advisers decided that the troubled king needed more than just a one-night stand with one of the many girls in his harem. Xerxes needed a companion! He needed a new queen!

Now as they began their search, those same advisers suggested a beauty contest. Isn't that just like a bunch of men? All the most beautiful maidens in Babylon were brought into the king's harem in the palace at Susa. Esther was also brought to the palace, but, following Mordecai's advice, kept her Jewish heritage a secret.

Esther 2:17 says, "Now the king was attracted to Esther more than to any of the other women." King Xerxes set the royal crown on Esther's head and declared her his queen. I told you she was a looker.

And that's where we pick up the story now. Sometime after Esther moved into the palace, King Xerxes made a fatal mistake by promoting a jerk named Haman to the No. 2 position in the land. Now Haman liked that move because, well, he had an ego the size of Kansas City! In fact, his first proclamation as No. 2 was that whenever he walked by, people couldn't just say, "Hi, Haman!" They were required to actually bow facedown to the ground.

Got any guesses as to who wasn't about to go there? Yeah, good ol' Uncle Mordecai. The only one he'd bow before was Jehovah. I mean, he was cordial, but he wasn't going to bow!

The Plot Thickens

Now Haman was anti-Semitic from the get-go, so Mordecai's refusal to bow was all the juice he needed to launch what was, essentially, an ancient holocaust. "Having learned who Mordecai's people were, he scorned the idea of killing only Mordecai. Instead Haman looked for a way to destroy all Mordecai's people, the Jews, throughout the whole kingdom of Xerxes" (3:6).

You can read about his plan in Esther 3, as Haman actually offers to chip in a bounty of about twenty million dollars to those who would carry out that evil deed before year's end.

The king, who did not know his new queen was a Jew, agreed to Haman's plan. The decree was sealed with the king's own signet ring and then distributed throughout the kingdom.

And when the people of Susa heard the decree, verse 15 says, the whole city was "bewildered."

PASSION AND PURPOSE

Now here's what I want you to track as we move through this story: had it not been for the passion and urgency of Mordecai and had it not been for the courageous sacrifice and personal involvement of Esther—two very ordinary people who had no choice but to shoulder this assignment—Haman's evil plot would have succeeded. The Jewish people would have been annihilated, and our Savior Jesus would never have been born.

Why did they do it? Why did they get involved? Why did they put their comfort and their personal welfare on the line? The answer is found in what I believe is the pivotal verse of this book: "And who knows but that you have come to royal position for such a time as this?" (4:14).

And so, driven by that sense of purpose—fueled by a firm conviction that this was God's great call on their lives—first Mordecai and then Esther moved out.

And the big takeaway from this story? Not only is it possible for one person to make a difference, but if that one person lives with purpose and with passion? That person will also possess world-changing power!

Now in the beginning of chapter four, Esther doesn't even have a clue what's going on. She has no idea that this holocaustic edict has been declared, because she's living in the protected environs of the palace.

But Uncle Mordy knew. And "when Mordecai learned of all that had been done, he tore his clothes, put on sackcloth and ashes, and went out into the city, wailing loudly and bitterly" (4:1).

And this was no act! Just pretend you're Jewish for a moment. And imagine what it would feel like to be so hated, your entire race is slated for execution. Picture the armbands and the yellow stars of David. Smell the putrid stench of death all around you. No wonder Mordecai wept.

"But he went only as far as the king's gate, because no one clothed in sackcloth was allowed to enter it. In every province to which the edict and order of the king came, there was great mourning among the Jews, with fasting, weeping and wailing. Many lay in sackcloth and ashes" (vv. 2, 3).

And do you know why? That's all they could do! They had no power! There was no person of access to plead their case! All they could do was mark off the calendar and wait.

But hold on. There was a method to Mordecai's passion. I think he positioned himself at just the right location so Esther would have to take note of him. And sure enough, "when Esther's maids and eunuchs came and told her about Mordecai, she was in great distress" (v. 4).

Because Esther loved Uncle Mordy, but she was also embarrassed by his outlandish display. So "she sent clothes for him to put on [*so he could come inside?*] . . . , but he would not accept them" (v. 4).

Why? Because this situation didn't call for polite social grace—it called for a determined and impassioned protest!

Mordecai said, in effect, "You need to feel the sting of my tears, Esther! And I want all of Susa to know there is a greater cause in play! So thanks, but no thanks. I'm staying right here!"

MAN'S FINEST HOUR

His passion reminds me of the late Vince Lombardi. This man held to such a passionate commitment for winning football games that he remains to this day the standard for what it means to be a coach. He poured his whole heart into his life's purpose, once saying, "I firmly believe that any man's finest hour—his greatest fulfillment to all he holds dear—is that moment when he has worked his heart out in a good cause and lies exhausted on the field of battle—victorious."[7]

Bart Starr says: "I wasn't mentally tough before I met Coach Lombardi. I hadn't reached the point where I refused to accept second best. I was too nice at times . . . but to win, you have to have a mental toughness. Coach Lombardi gave me that. He taught me that you must have a flaming desire to win. It's got to dominate all your waking hours. It can't ever wane. It's got to glow in you all the time."[8]

TRADING PLACES

Lombardi put it this way: "The only way to succeed at anything is to give it everything."[9]

And that's what Mordecai was doing. "No, Esther, I'm *not* coming inside. And if I offend and embarrass you? Get over it! I'm on a mission and I will not quit!"

I heard about a woman in Mobile, Alabama, who took her son to the grocery store. She set him in the seat of the cart and started up the aisle, and as she began making her selections, her little boy spotted a huge stack of chocolate chip cookies.

He said, "Mom! Can I have some chocolate chip cookies?"

"No, you can't," she said. "And I told you before we came in not to beg for everything you see!"

She started up the next aisle, and the kid wailed, "Can I have just a couple of chocolate chip cookies?"

"No! Now sit down!"

Halfway up the next aisle the kid pleaded again, "Mama, can I have just one chocolate chip cookie?"

"I said NO!" She completed her rounds and brought the cart to a stop at the checkout line, only to notice her son, no more than three years old, slowly rise out of the cart seat, turn his big brown eyes toward Heaven, and shout at the top of his lungs, "In the naaaame of Jeeeesusss! Give me some cookies!"

She said everybody in the store started cheering and clapping. Others went back to the cookie aisle, and by the time she was loading her groceries, her son had been given twenty-three boxes of chocolate chip cookies.

Now while I have some serious problems with the kid's methodology (not to mention his theology), I'm thrilled with his passion. That kid knew how to get things done!

Do you understand that passion always elicits a response? Passion excites and exhilarates. It inflames and incites the masses to action! And if a leader is passionately committed? He will prompt that same commitment in his people.

I can't help but wonder how many times Esther stood at the window, watching Mordecai, strangely drawn to his troubled spirit. And even though she didn't understand what he was doing, much less why, she was hooked. Somehow, someway, she was going to find out.

That's why "Esther summoned Hathach, one of the king's eunuchs assigned to attend her, and ordered him to find out what was troubling Mordecai and why" (v. 5).

In other words, "Why won't he take the clothing I sent him? Why won't he just come in and talk to me? What's so tragic that he keeps weeping all the time?"

"So Hathach went out to Mordecai. . . . Mordecai told him everything that had happened to him, including the exact amount of money Haman had promised to pay into the royal treasury for the destruction of the Jews. He also gave him a copy of the text of the edict for their annihilation, which had been published in Susa, to show to Esther and explain it to her" (vv. 6-8).

JUST THE FACTS

I mean, was Mordecai ready or what? He had all the documents, folks. "Here it is, Esther. Right here in black and white, girl. If you don't believe me, read it for yourself."

Please take note of Mordecai's careful attention to detail. There was no exaggeration, no cooking the books, no hearsay, no third-hand information. Just the facts, ma'am.

Speaking of the facts, I have in my files an AP report. It seems that a Linda Burnett, age twenty-three, had gone to a supermarket to pick up some groceries.

Several people noticed she was sitting in her car with the windows rolled up and her eyes closed, with both hands clasped behind the back of her head.

One customer, who'd been in the store about an hour, noticed that Linda was in the same position she'd been in when he went inside. So he walked over to her car and noted that her eyes were now open, but she looked very strange.

He asked her if she was OK, and she said that she'd been shot in the back of the head and had been holding her brain in for over an hour. The man called 911, and the paramedics broke into the car because the doors were locked and Linda refused to remove her hands from her head.

When they finally got in, they discovered that Linda had a wad of bread dough on the back of her head. It seems that a can of biscuits had exploded due to the heat, making a huge noise that sounded like a gunshot, and the wad of dough hit her smack in the back of the head! So when she reached back to find out what happened, she felt the dough and thought it was her brain!

That's when she passed out, then recovered and tried to hold in her brain till finally someone came and helped her!

Don't you see? Passion is powerful stuff, but make sure you get your facts straight! Before you get everybody in an uproar, take the time to see if it really is gray matter or just a crescent roll. Like the commercial says, "Don't judge too quickly!" Get the facts!

Mordecai instinctively understood this was a crucial moment in Israel's history. If he was to have any success at all, he'd better do his homework!

And that's why, with an intensity born out of the need, Mordecai gave Hathach the facts (say that three times), "and he told him to urge her to go into the king's presence to beg for mercy and plead with him for her people" (v. 8).

The sackcloth was the bait, and now Uncle Mordy is settin' the hook, folks! Tell Esther to do something about this!

So "Hathach went back and reported to Esther what Mordecai had said. Then she instructed him to say to Mordecai, 'All the king's officials and the people of the royal provinces know that for any man or woman who approaches the king in the inner court without being summoned the king has but one law: that he be put to death. The only exception to this is for the king to extend the gold scepter to him and spare his life. But thirty days have passed since I was called to go to the king'" (vv. 9-11).

AN ANCIENT CLICKER

Granted, that's not your normal marital relationship, but that's the way it was for royalty in Persia. If Esther showed up uninvited, her hubby had to extend the scepter! (Which, I figure, was an ancient prototype of the remote control: *Click.* "Honey, let's talk.") Otherwise, Esther would be killed.

"But Uncle Mordy? The king hasn't called for me, so I can't see him! And if I try—I could die!"

"Esther's words were reported to Mordecai" (v. 12), and now Mordecai is faced with a dilemma. I mean, he loved Esther! And he probably wondered, *Should I back off or keep pushing? I know she's uncomfortable . . . I'M uncomfortable! And if I press the case, it could cost her—her life! She respects me, and I don't want to abuse that trust. So do I back off and say, "It's all right, we'll figure something out," or do I press the point: "Esther, you've got to do this!"*

Well, Mordecai had a clear vision of his calling, so he pressed the point with Esther, "Do not think that because you are in the king's house you alone of all the Jews will escape" (v. 13).

"Because, Esther, beneath that crown is a Jewish head. And if you pass on this? You'll die with the rest of us!"

"If you remain silent at this time, relief and deliverance for the Jews will arise from another place" (v. 14).

"Help will come from somewhere because God gave our nation a promise. And that promise has not yet been fulfilled. We still have a purpose, and God will see to it that His purpose is accomplished. This deal isn't dependent on you, Esther. It'll happen with or without you, but if you don't get involved 'you and your father's family will perish'" (v. 14).

And then he said it. May I have a drumroll?

"And who knows but that you have come to royal position for such a time as this?" (v. 14).

WHO KNOWS?

Isn't that about the greatest line you've ever heard? "Esther, maybe this is why I adopted you. And why God wanted me to raise you as my own! Maybe it's why I poured my life into you and modeled before you an impassioned commitment to God! Maybe this has been His plan for your life all along! Maybe it's why you became queen—a Jewess on a Gentile throne? I don't think so! So get with it, Esther! Trade in some of that beauty for just one ounce of bravery . . . OK?"

I think of Churchill, who in May 1939, was called to the royal palace and asked to mobilize the military against Hitler. He humbly accepted the job, and that night he wrote in his journal, "I went to bed and I felt as if I were walking with destiny. And that all my past life had been but a preparation for this hour and this trial."

Churchill sensed that his life had finally reached its purpose, that God had called him for this perilous moment. And it was that sense of purpose that emboldened him to stand before a war-torn, frightened nation and say, "I have nothing to offer but blood, toil, sweat and tears."

He added, "Death and sorrow will be the companions of our journey. Hardship our garments. Constancy and valor our only shield. We must be united. We must be undaunted. We must be inflexible."

Just after France had surrendered, he told the House of Commons, "Let us therefore brace ourselves to our duties and so bear ourselves that, if the British Empire and its Commonwealth last for a thousand years, men will say, "This was their finest hour.""[10]

One man passionately committed to his purpose—and he held an entire nation together.

In that same way Esther, despite the pounding of her heart and that inner voice of fear shouting, "There's no way I can do this," somehow managed to hear the voice of God. The only question was, what would she do about it? The ball was obviously in her court.

Between verse 14 and verse 15 are the unwritten lines of a young woman deciding her destiny. She's taking a gut check, folks. Will she put her life on the line, or will she bail? Will she put off even her own life, or will she cling to her crown?

Finally . . .

"Esther sent this reply to Mordecai: 'Go, gather together all the Jews who are in Susa, and fast for me. Do not eat or drink for three days, night or day. I and my maids will fast as you do'" (v. 16).

"If we're going to do this, we're grounding it in prayer first." How wise was that? Then she says it: "When this is done, I will go to the king, even though it is against the law. And if I perish, I perish" (v. 16).

Wow! She could have played it safe. There's no reason to believe Xerxes would ever know her true race! She could have opted for the path of least resistance. But this woman was so impacted by God's purpose that she says, "I'm going for it! My whole life has been preparation for this. So if in the process of doing it, I die? So be it!"

DOING THE DEED

Esther realized that her duty was to obey the prompting of her heart, to trust in God's wisdom and timing and direction. And if that required that she go right into the belly of hardship, suffering, and possibly even death—it was what it was. At least she'd be where God wanted her to be, and for Esther, that was enough!

But she moved out on more than emotion. Esther prayed and fasted for three days. If she was going to do this, she needed all the strength of Heaven itself. And only then did this brave girl kick it into gear. Do you see it? "On the third day Esther put on her royal robes . . ." (5:1).

She got all dolled up—taking full advantage of all that beauty God had given her—and then she "stood in the inner court of the palace, in front of the king's hall" (v. 1). Right where the king would be sitting and where he couldn't possibly *not* see her.

And sure enough, "the king was sitting on his royal throne in the hall, facing the entrance" (v. 1).

Meanwhile, Esther's heart was doing a drum solo. I mean, what would he do? How would he respond to her bold, uninvited advance?

"When he saw Queen Esther standing in the court, he was pleased with her and held out to her the gold scepter that was in his hand. So Esther [*breathing a sigh of relief and thinking, OK, I'm not dead yet*] approached and touched the tip of the scepter" (v. 2). Do you know what she was saying when she did that? She was acknowledging the king's authority!

You may have noticed that most king-types kind of like people who acknowledge their kingliness, am I right? Whether it's your boss or your biggest client, whether it's the head of your civic organization or the senior pastor of your church, kings tend to really like it when people bow to their power!

Christian Herter, former governor of Massachusetts, tells of the time he was running for a second term. After a busy morning and no lunch, he arrived at a church barbecue and was famished. Approaching the serving line, he held out his plate to the woman serving the chicken. She put one piece on his plate and turned to the next person in line.

"Excuse me," Governor Herter said. "Could I have another piece of chicken?"

"Sorry," said the woman, "I'm only supposed to give one piece of chicken to each person."

"But I'm starved," the governor said.

"Sorry, only one to a customer."

Since the governor was really hungry, he decided to throw some weight around. "Lady, do you know who I am? I am the governor of this state."

"Do you know who I am?" the woman replied. "I'm the lady in charge of the chicken. Now move along!"

Now Esther was, after all, the queen and the most beautiful woman in the land. And the king obviously had a deep and abiding affection for her. But Esther seemed to understand this wasn't about her ego; this was about her life's purpose. And so, ego in check, she reached out and touched his scepter with a gracious, quiet humility.

"The king asked, 'What is it, Queen Esther? What is your request? Even up to half the kingdom, it will be given you'" (v. 3).

Wow! Talk about a confirmation of God's leadership! "I'll give you half of everything I own, girl! Just name it!"

So she did. "If it pleases the king," replied Esther, "let the king, together with Haman, come today to a banquet I have prepared for him" (v. 4).

The king and Haman were pleased to attend Esther's banquet. But she didn't bring up the problem with the king's decree right away. Instead, Esther requested the pleasure of their company at a banquet the following day as well.

TABLE FOR THREE

The king and Haman accepted Esther's invitation, and together they "went to dine with Queen Esther, and as they were drinking wine on that second day, the king again asked, 'Queen Esther, what is your petition? It will be given you. What is your request? Even up to half the kingdom, it will be granted.'

"Then Queen Esther answered, 'If I have found favor with you, O king, and if it pleases your majesty, grant me my life—this is my petition. And spare my people—this is my request. For I and my people have been sold for destruction and slaughter and annihilation. If we had merely been sold as male and female slaves, I would have kept quiet, because no such distress would justify disturbing the king'" (7:1-4). In other words, "We've been slaves before and we could handle that. But this is death!"

"King Xerxes asked Queen Esther, 'Who is he? Where is the man who has dared to do such a thing?'

"Esther said, "The adversary and enemy is this vile Haman'" (vv. 5, 6).

Guess what happened next? By nightfall, Haman was hanged. The king empowered Esther to write a new decree, allowing the Jews to defend themselves and take revenge upon their enemies. Esther's people were saved!

Had she been able to anticipate Xerxes' response, this would have been a cakewalk! But for all Esther knew, the king would say, "No, honey, Haman's valuable to me despite this evil deed. Off with her head!" But to Esther that didn't matter. Because she obviously believed, "This cause is greater than my life!" (See Esther 4:16.)

Strange words in our culture.

CULTURAL DISCONNECT

We live in a culture of absurdity. Life is a bad joke . . . and nothing really matters. There's nothing worth living for and nothing worth dying for. Life is a pain . . . then you die. No one cares about anyone else. No one is willing to stand up for his convictions. There is no cause worthy of sacrifice!

But our culture is wrong, people. There is something worth living for—and yes, dying for. And who knows but that maybe your whole life has been nothing more than preparation for God's present call.

Could it be that your whole life has been but a prologue for this unique moment?

Could it be?

The story is told of a woman who was committed to a psychiatric hospital. After she was admitted, she asked the staff for a large piece of canvas and lots of paint, which they readily supplied.

Months later, she invited the staff to watch the unveiling of her "life's work." As she dramatically pulled back the sheet covering her masterpiece, she revealed a canvas with not one paint stroke on it. Everyone sat there, politely "admiring" the would-be painting. Finally, the chief administrator asked, "What is it? Tell us about your painting."

She replied, "It's the children of Israel crossing the Red Sea."

Everyone in the group was puzzled but acted as though he understood.

The administrator asked, "Where's the Red Sea?"

"Oh, it's already parted. Half is on one side of the canvas and half on the other."

"Well, where are the children of Israel?"

The woman said, "Oh, they've already gone through."

"But what about the Egyptian army?"

"Oh, they haven't arrived yet."

What a shame. Can you imagine having lived your whole life without making even one mark on your canvas?

Let me ask it another way. Can you imagine living your life without ever seizing God's greater purpose—and the very reason why you breathe?

Don't let that happen to you. Waiting time is not wasted time. Instead, like Esther, look at the whole of your life as merely God's preparation for "such a time as this." Seize His great challenge for your life.

Come on, put some real strokes on that canvas. And make your life God's masterpiece.

CHAPTER 9

TRADING POTENTIAL FOR PASSION

SOME TIME AGO I was asked to speak to a group of Christian men on the topic of prayer. But not just any kind of prayer. I was asked to address the topic of *manly* prayer. And in case I didn't know what that meant, I was instructed not to talk in a manner that was either sensitive or emotional.

Not sure what to do with that, I pretended I needed to check my schedule: "I'll have to get back to you."

Thinking maybe I'd missed something in all my years of studying Scripture, I immediately pulled out my concordance and did a word search. Guess what? I was shocked. The phrase *manly prayer* isn't in there! Neither is the word *manly*.

Then I remembered my instructions about being neither sensitive nor emotional. So I thought, *Maybe I should read some of the famous prayers in the Bible. Maybe they'll have some manly insight I've never seen before.*

So I read Jacob's prayer in Genesis 32. Jacob was headed back to his homeland, where years before he had tricked his brother, Esau, and stolen his birthright. Jacob said, "Save me, I pray, from the hand of my brother Esau, for I am afraid" (v. 11). Well, that one didn't help because fear is an emotion, and I wasn't supposed to be emotional.

Before Samson was born, his daddy prayed for a sign, saying, "O Lord, I beg you" (Judges 13:8). But begging isn't manly! Then Samson, during his swan song, prayed, "O Sovereign LORD, remember me. O God, please strengthen me just once more" (16:28). Does that sound a little whiney to anybody besides me? Buck up, Samson! Either topple the place or shut yer yapper!

And what about Elijah? After a confrontation with evil King Ahab, Elijah was so depressed the Bible says "he came to a broom tree, sat down under it and prayed that he might die. 'I have had enough, LORD,' he said. 'Take my life'" (1 Kings 19:4). Big baby.

Hezekiah was deathly ill and had been told he would not recover. He "turned his face to the wall and prayed" (2 Kings 20:2). And then he "wept bitterly" (v. 3).

And consider Jesus: On the night before He was crucified, the Bible says Jesus "began to be sorrowful and troubled." And He even admitted those emotions to His men, saying, "My soul is overwhelmed with sorrow to the point of death." Then, He "fell with his face to the ground and prayed, 'My Father, if it is possible, may this cup be taken from me'" (Matthew 26:37-39). Scripture says He was in "anguish," and began praying even "more earnestly," to the point that His sweat became "like drops of blood falling to the ground" (Luke 22:44).

About then I closed my Bible and thought, *I'm not sure what to do with this assignment.*

DITCHING MANLY PRAYER

I mean, I'm sorry, but prayer is, at its core, emotional! It's passionate! Or, as the Bible puts it, earnest. The psalmist said, "O God, you are my God, earnestly I seek you" (63:1). James said, "The earnest prayer of a righteous person has great power." (James 5:16, NLT). So tell me, how do you give a talk on prayer and yet leave "earnest" out of it?

Not only that, prayer is also undignified and downright *un*manly, at least as we understand the word. When Moses prayed for Israel's sin, he "lay prostrate before the LORD those forty days and forty nights" (Deuteronomy 9:25). *Prostrate* means face to the ground—which is pretty much the same position you take when you've got issues with your prostate, right?

When Paul and Silas were in jail, they prayed and sang praise songs until well past midnight. Now check this out: two grown men, all alone in a dark, secluded room, in the middle of the night, singing? Talk about a scandal in the making!

Listen, prayer isn't manly! At least, not in the way we think of manliness. But that's the problem. Man, in his fallen state, is way too concerned about projecting just how manly he can be. And I can go there, too. I can grunt and scratch and make body noises with the best of 'em.

The problem is, man in his fallen state is far less "man" than God intended him to be. And that's why we male-types tend to compensate so much. We're trying to cover over our true selves: the fact that I don't have life wired and I've got flat sides I'd rather you not see. I hide those things from you by discussing box scores and trash-talking during pickup games. But deep inside? I'm know I'm not all that.

But in the world of fallen man, there's nothing more frightening, nothing more potentially mind-blowing, than to actually admit it.

And yet, admitting it is exactly what prayer is! And "manly prayer"? Hey, the most manly prayer I know came from the lips of Jesus. His heart was absolutely broken, yet He told the Father, "Not my will, but yours be done" (Luke 22:42). Hey, it takes a real man not to react the way you want to react. It takes a real man to do what needs to be done, no matter how undignified that vital task may be.

Are you tracking with me? True manliness isn't about scratching, grunting, and doing high fives. It's about being strong enough to admit that you are neither all-sufficient nor totally together—and smart enough to acknowledge you don't know it all . . . and never will.

I remembered the "manly prayer" incident when I was reading from Matthew 4 recently. As I read the account of how Jesus selected the men who would serve as His management team, I was amazed all over again.

Amazed, because when Jesus searched out His key leaders? He didn't go headhunting in Jerusalem's business district. He didn't conduct a Trump-style apprentice approach, either. Jesus went to Galilee. He went to Redneck, Knee-Jerk, Hayseed Central. And He came alongside of group hard-edged, rough-hewn, tough-talking fishermen.

You want to talk about manly men? These guys were not the crowd to be messing with, if you get my drift. Yet . . . Jesus messed with them. He'd seen them hanging around on the fringes of His ministry, so He came to them. "Come, follow me," Jesus said, "and I will make you fishers of men" (Matthew 4:19).

I can just hear what Jesus was thinking: *I realize what you're doing is important. This isn't just a hobby—this is your livelihood, and it's supper on the table for most all of Palestine! But I've got a bigger catch in mind for you than just a net full of tilapia!*

And I'm convinced that you men are just the tribe that can pull it off. See, I want you to do two things:

I want you to come. I want you to follow. And then, when you're ready, I want you to . . . go fish. But this time, I want you to fish for people. So as you follow, I will build in you all the necessary skills you'll need to go fish. I will empower you to attract people to faith with every bit as much skill as you now attract fish with bait.

So come! Follow!

COME, FOLLOW . . . GO FISH

Verse 20 says, "At once they left their nets and followed him."

All told, twelve manly men were called to form this man-fishing band. But in this passage, only four are specifically mentioned. And of those four, I want to focus on just one.

I want to talk to you about John.

That may surprise you, given the "manly" theme I've already laid out because, let's face it, the common view of John, with regard to machismo, is kind of mixed.

Yeah, he was a member of Jesus' management team. And yeah, he also wrote several books in the New Testament. And yeah, he was a strong leader in the church at Jerusalem.

But . . . John also had two mamas. One biological mom and one other "mom" he later adopted (see John 19:27). Any flags waving yet? Not only that, but John was a tender sort. He was the disciple who, while reclining next to Jesus near the low table at the last supper, leaned back against Jesus' chest to talk to him (see John 13:22-25). He was the one who stood with the women the day Jesus was crucified (see John 19:26). And most damning of all? John's the one described in Scripture as "the disciple whom Jesus loved" (John 13:23).

Do I have to tell you what some people in our depraved culture have done with that phrase? I mean, when a couple of grown men are described as "loving each other" and they're "reclining" at the table side by side? That's more than enough to raise an eyebrow and cast a questioning glance.

"I mean, what's up with this John dude? Because . . . Peter? He was manly! I like Peter! But John? He's kind of soft, don't you think?" Which is why, throughout the ages, John has been tagged—inaccurately and unfortunately—as a metrosexual-type disciple.

JOHN'S NOT-SO-OBVIOUS POTENTIAL

But when Jesus first met him, far from some mild-mannered Clark Kent type, John was a tough, foul-mouthed fisherman, a card-carrying member of the Angry Man Club.

One time he and his brother James tried to destroy an entire city just because they couldn't get a room at the Motel 6.

And in Luke 9, they were sent on a mission, but nobody would listen. So they stomped back to Jesus and said, "Rabbi, those people wouldn't believe us! Let's torch the place!"

Another time, a huge crowd had gathered, and the people were hungry. What was John's solution? "Let 'em find their own food!"

I believe it was John's inner core of sensitivity that caused him to become so angry. Living with an angry older brother, barely clinging to the bottom rung on the ladder of the family business, working alongside tough-minded, hard-living fishermen—John had probably been pushed around and put down his entire life. So that, in time, refusing to knuckle under to that abuse, John copped an attitude and gave back as good as he got.

People, John had a raging temper. I'm not saying that was some kind of disqualifier, because it's not. I mean, can you name even one person who doesn't have a flat side? *Any*body who's free from all deficiencies or idiosyncrasies that might make them less than the ideal catch?

I think Jesus saw something in John nobody else seemed to see. I'm no psychologist, but I did stay at a Holiday Inn Express last night, and I'm convinced that most men who suffer from Angry Man Syndrome are, at the core, pretty much like John. They're fairly sensitive guys, maybe even insecure—they just don't want you to know it. They think, *But I'm tired of getting hurt and I don't like being messed with!* So what do they do? They adopt the tough-guy drill. You know, *I'm going to give it to you before you give it to me.* And because that's the way men have done it for centuries, it's assumed that's the way men *should* do it . . . right?

That's evidently what John thought. Until he encountered the one man in history who really *did* know what it means to act like a man. And sure enough, John, having watched Jesus in action for three years and having eaten with Him and worked for Him and listened to Him and traveled beside Him . . . John, in time, learned that true manliness is being strong, without needing to be mean.

JESUS SAW SOMETHING

Jesus saw something in John nobody else could see. He loved seeing potential in people and displaying His amazing glory in "losers" others had tossed aside. He loved shaping nobodies into somebodies! He took the weak and made them strong; He transformed the rebellious into humble servants. He took people as they were and transformed them into what, one day—through the power of God—they could become!

Jesus took one look at Peter and saw a powerful spokesman for the gospel. Kind of flighty? Yeah. Impulsive and erratic?

Definitely. A gift for exaggeration? We all know that's true. Yet, there was just something about that guy.

When Jesus met Andrew, He saw a future evangelist. Kind of quiet? Yeah. Almost introvertish? Sure! Yet after spending time with Jesus, guess what? Every time you find Andrew in Scripture, he's bringing yet somebody else to come meet Jesus.

So why should it surprise us that when Jesus saw John, He saw a man of enduring, inner strength. Kind of sensitive? Yep. He covered it with a snarly attitude, but he was at the core a very tender soul, the type Peter could grind into mincemeat if he wanted. And yet he was the kind of man who—with just a little help from Jesus—could become a real anchor for the faith, a to-the-death kind of follower who would stay at a task when everybody else, including Peter, had already cut and run.

Last Man Standing

It's true. John wasn't at all like Peter. Not at all the step-up-to-the-mic face guy who could deliver the Pentecost sermon with the power such a moment required (see Acts 2:14-40). But you know what? What John *could* do . . . John did.

That's why Jesus affirmed to John that there was a place for him on Jesus' first team. And the truth is, John would be the last man standing when all the others ran for cover.

Now aren't you glad Jesus didn't demand that John act like Peter, or James, or any of the others? He wanted John to reflect God's glory exactly as God had wired John to be.

Besides, it was Peter who tested Jesus' patience (see Matthew 16:23; Mark 8:33), but it was John that Jesus loved.

And that's what I love about Jesus.

Good leader that He was, He knew that everyone contributes differently and that there's no one right way to get things done.

Now listen, those who don't do that? Who practice an autocratic style? You know, it's *my* way or the highway? They'll lose every time they compete against someone who accepts people as they are (and where they are), building on their own innate personalities and shaping them into whatever God (not the boss) wants them to be.

If everybody looked, talked, and acted the same, our world would be like an Osmond family Christmas special. The kind of leadership Jesus modeled requires the ability to affirm uniqueness, to seek out previously untapped talent, and then to challenge people to channel those abilities in the direction of their God-given potential.

The problem is, we don't do that very well. We tend to be drawn to people like ourselves, right? At least I do. You know why? Because I'm normal! And if only everybody else would just shape up and get it together—you know, like me?—we could get things done!

But don't you find it a bit strange that nobody in your life is normal but you? Isn't it odd that everybody you know is a weirdly mutated wacko—except you?

Hey, if Peter really was *the* consummate disciple, then why did Jesus go ahead and choose eleven more? If Peter really was *the* prototype, why mess with perfection?

I'll tell you why. It's because nobody has the complete package. We all have our strengths, but we all also have our weaknesses.

Some people are introverts, and all the extroverts make fun of 'em. Some people are dreamers, much to the consternation of the bottom-liners. Some folks are artistic by nature—while others can hit a softball 473 miles—on a clothesline. But who's to say one is any better than the other?

Certainly not Jesus. And that's why when He put together His team, Jesus picked eleven; He didn't just pick one.

The Animal School

Steven Covey, in *The Seven Habits of Highly Effective People,* illustrated his sixth habit, "Synergize," with an often-quoted little story written by educator R. H. Reeves. It's called "The Animal School."

Once upon a time, the animals decided they must do something heroic to meet the problems of a "New World," so they organized a school. They adopted an activity curriculum consisting of running, climbing, swimming and flying. To make it easier to administer, all the animals took all the subjects.

The duck was excellent in swimming, better in fact than his instructor, and made excellent grades in flying, but was very poor in running. Since he was low in running he had to stay after school and also drop swimming to practice running. This was kept up until his web feet were badly worn and he was only average in swimming. But average was acceptable in school, so nobody worried about that except the duck.

The rabbit started at the top of his class in running, but had a nervous breakdown because of so much makeup in swimming.

The squirrel was excellent in climbing until he developed frustrations in the flying class where his teacher made him start from the ground up instead of from the tree-top down. He also developed charley horses from over-exertion and got a C in climbing and a D in running.

The eagle was a problem child and had to be disciplined severely. In climbing class he beat all the others to the top, but insisted on using his own method of getting there.

At the end of the year, an abnormal eel that could swim exceedingly well and also could run, climb and fly a little had the highest overall average and graduated valedictorian.[1]

Do you get the point? It's entirely OK for you to just be you, to celebrate the fact that you're wired exactly as God intended you to be wired.

So the great challenge of your life is not to be re-created into somebody else's image for you, but for you to be the best *you* you can be!

I don't mean that you ought to be impervious to change, or that you're fine just as you are and that you have no need for any kind of self-improvement. I'm not saying that!

Of course, there are adjustments you should make! Just as there were adjustments John needed to make—not to mention the rest of that crowd.

I mean, Philip needed to be less obsessed with numbers and more impressed with God. Andrew needed to trust more than his own instincts—he needed to trust Jesus! Peter needed to listen more than he spoke. And John? He needed to get over being angry and just be the man God made him to be.

And Jesus was deeply committed to seeing those changes happen, but—and here's the key—He affirmed each disciple for the unique person he already was.

See, if you really love someone, you want him to become all he can be. But then again, if you really love him—what he is right now is OK, too.

Of course, Jesus stretched John, but He did it in a context of acceptance. There was never a moment when John had to wonder, *What's Jesus thinking about me? Is there something I need to do to make sure He still accepts me?*

None of that ever happened on Jesus' team.

MOLDING A MAN OF PASSION

Instead, Jesus brought John from where he was to where he needed to be, in an atmosphere of love. Even more, He adjusted His methods for stretching John according to John's unique personality.

Here's what I mean. A man of passion (like John) can easily be abused. You can tap into that wholehearted passion that so obviously drives him, and you can wring out of that dude everything you think you need. Then when he's wrung dry? You can just toss him aside and find another victim.

Although Jesus could have done that to John, He didn't.

Instead, He ministered to John (and the others) according to a principle I'm really trying to cultivate. Jesus viewed His men, not in terms of "What can that person do for me?" but rather, "What can I do for him?"

Because true leadership is not about manipulating people. It's not about pushing your agenda or putting people down or using your role or record of achievement as some subtle, yet effective, hammer.

Manipulation controls people, obligates people, and takes advantage of people by unfair and unscrupulous means. And manipulation is usually practiced by insecure people who try to look superior by making other people squirm. Such tactics are not usually done in a bold, up-front manner, but behind closed doors. Or with subtle hints and well-timed sarcasm.

When I was in Kentucky for a meeting, I had breakfast with a man who is quite wealthy. Which means he's been used (and I mean *used*) by a host of Christian organizations. They wanted to use his prestigious name on their letterheads. They spent time with him because he had money—and they got a lot of it. They used his time, which he gave without reserve until, in time, these Christian organizations practically decimated my friend's life. His marriage is destroyed. His son is in trouble with the law. And my friend's been trying to cope by abusing alcohol. Today, not one member of his family wants anything to do with Jesus Christ or the church. Why? Because he was used—rode hard and put up wet. Everybody, especially Christian leaders, used to him to perform a vital function and fulfill an important kingdom need. But nobody ever looked to him as somebody who had needs, too.

That's *not* how Jesus got the job done. I want to show you two vignettes from Jesus' encounters with John, each revealing the personal and tender way Jesus carefully ministered to him. And please note—Jesus *ministered* to John; He did not *manipulate* John.

Grabbing for the Throne

The first scene is a rather disturbing encounter between Jesus and John's mother. According to Matthew 20:20, she "came to Jesus with her sons and, kneeling down, asked a favor of him." Now John's mom was Salome. And according to Scripture, Salome was with Mary, the mother of Jesus, when Jesus was on the cross. Which is fitting because Salome was Mary's sister (see Mark 15:40, John 19:25; also Matthew 4:21; 27:56). So what we have here is Jesus' aunt asking Jesus for a favor. Yet, she bows at His feet! Most aunts don't do that when they greet their nephews, but Salome's layin' it on thick, baby! Jesus asked, "What is it you want?" She said, "Grant that one of these two sons of mine may sit at your right and the other at your left in your kingdom" (v. 21).

Now don't be too hard on her. After all, she's a good Jewish mother. She's proud of her boys. And since Jesus just said that all twelve are gettin' a throne, I can hear her thinking, *Why not give the best seats to Your cousins, Jesus? Obviously, You deserve the center seat, but can Jimmy and Johnny have the next two? After all, Jesus, we're family!*

"You don't know what you are asking," Jesus said. "Can you drink the cup I am going to drink?"

I don't think they had a clue what Jesus was saying. I think they were so blinded by ambition, they would have said anything if it meant grabbing that throne! "'We can,' they answered" (v. 22).

Jesus said, "You will indeed drink from my cup, but to sit at my right or left is not for me to grant. These places belong to those for whom they have been prepared by my Father" (v. 23).

Matthew says that when the other disciples heard what John's mama asked, they were indignant! Do you know why? They were ticked because James and John thought to ask before *they* thought to ask! That's why!

I don't want to do a hatchet job on these guys, but people— Jesus' disciples were as selfish and greedy and competitive as any team of coworkers could be!

And even though Jesus constantly warned them about beatings and floggings—and foxes with holes and birds with nests— they didn't get it. They didn't leave behind family and career just to watch their beloved leader die in disgrace! They had signed up for future glory and all the perks reserved for the powerful!

Remember Peter's question to the Lord? "We have left everything to follow you! What then will there be for us?" (Matthew 19:27). What he really wanted to know was, "What will there be . . . for me?" He didn't care about them. And they didn't care about him. It was all about *me*!

Reaching for the Towel

The second scene happens in Matthew 18, when the disciples came asking Jesus, "Who is the greatest in the kingdom?" (v. 1). "I mean, besides You. Who's #2?" Luke says an argument had ensued. The disciples were engaged in a seething, volatile discussion as to which of them was second in line after Jesus. Truth is, they'd already voted, and it came back a twelve-way tie!

Such competition continued all the way to the cross. Even on the night Jesus was betrayed, the entire dinner conversation was yet another discussion concerning who was the greatest in the kingdom.

And that's why Jesus grabbed the towel. Because Peter didn't get it. Andrew didn't get it. Judas obviously didn't get it. Then again, neither did the one guy Jesus thought just might get it. Not even John understood.

So Jesus, having already taught this principle many times (and by this time He was no more than twelve hours away from the cross), slipped away from the table, drew some water, wrapped a towel around His waist, and began the humble, undignified task of washing His disciples' dirty feet (see John 13:4, 5). And even as He knelt before that first set of dirty toes, the disciples were still at it: which of us is the greatest?

Till they heard the sound of splashing water. That's when everyone realized, there's an elephant in here! Here we are, arguing about who gets to sit where—debating about who'll be #2 when #1 gets His glory—yet #1 is doing the very thing He said *we* should have done.

Do you recall what Jesus said right after John's mama asked about seating assignments? And anybody remember who it was He said it to? Not just James and John. No, Jesus directed His rebuke to His entire team.

By the way, that's another beautiful thing about Jesus' ministry style. Whatever He said to one of His men, He said to all of His men. It's true . . . Jesus recruited individuals, but He trained them as a team. And that's a lesson all of us could profit from.

So even though John was His primary focus, Jesus said to all of 'em, "You know that the rulers of the Gentiles lord it over them, and their high officials exercise authority over them. Not so with you. Instead, whoever wants to become great among you must be your servant, and whoever wants to be first must be your slave—just as the Son of Man did not come to be served, but to serve, and to give his life as a ransom for many" (Matthew 20:25-28).

Back in the upper room, it's the night before His death—but they still didn't get it! So does Jesus blow a fuse? Does He threaten and cajole and harass and harangue them?

No! Instead, while they're busy grabbing for the throne, Jesus humbly—and with great love—reached for the towel.

CHRIST'S CONSISTENT EXAMPLE

It's moments like that, I'm convinced, that forever marked John's heart. If you've ever wondered why Jesus made such an impact on His disciples? There's an answer: because everything Christ said was always reinforced by what He did. His was an impeccably consistent example. He didn't just talk serving; Jesus served.

Can you imagine watching Jesus in action? Not for just a brief glimpse or a handful of momentary encounters. But night and day . . . for three years!

Think of it: no one executed the Great Exchange more effectively than Jesus. When He came to earth, He set aside all the glories of Heaven for the indignities of humanity. Then He waited—waited patiently, for God's perfect moment when His salvation would finally be revealed.

He Put Off "equality with God" (Philippians 2:6) and Put On the "nature of a servant," making "himself nothing" (v. 7).

And He feverishly maintained a vital connection with the Father—even in the most intense moments of His life—saying, "Father, if you are willing, take this cup from me; yet not my will, but yours be done" (Luke 22:42). A powerful example of the *X* Factor.

And nobody watched Jesus more closely than John.

He'd spent day and night for three years with the most loving yet utterly manly man this world has ever known—a man who was also the most giving, most kind, most servant-hearted leader to ever wear the leadership mantle.

One minute Jesus was rebuking His men for their pride, and the next, He was washing their feet—without a harsh word or any suggestion that they should wash His in return. What love! What a sensitive and passionate man!

Jesus—constantly pressed by so many needs, yet always willing to cradle a child. Jesus—the object of so many pleas for His attention, yet scooping a dead girl into His arms and giving her back her life. Why, Jesus even embraced a man with leprosy, the social outcast of His day, whom everybody else called "unclean."

Matthew 9 says that whenever Jesus saw large crowds of people, He was moved to the point of upset. He knew their lost, wandering condition. And it made Him ill.

When His friend Lazarus died, Jesus wept—openly . . . loudly, even to the point of snorting like a horse.[2]

When Jesus prayed in the garden, His passion was so strong He actually sweat huge drops of blood.

In John 1:14, Jesus is described as the "Word" that "became flesh and made his dwelling among us." Can there be any doubt? Jesus was the greatest collection of flesh the world has ever known. And you can't follow someone like that—you cannot walk in His footsteps—and *not* be impacted by His sensitive ways.

So I ask you, how could John *not* become more sensitive and responsive to the needs of others? How could he *not* become a man of incredible, awe-inspiring love as he stayed close to Jesus and learned of Him—as he applied the *X* Factor?

But understand: John didn't fundamentally alter his very personality. He simply moved from being a passionate, angry man to being a passionate . . . man of love.

And if you were to ask him how it happened? His answer would go something like this: "I love Him because He first loved me" (see 1 John 4:19).

TOUGH-HEARTED JOHN

Now that's probably way too much love talk for manly men to try to swallow. But hear me now: don't you dare question John's manhood. I couldn't. When I trace the history of his life, I find more strength of character, more loyalty, more personal courage in him than in all the other disciples put together.

Did you know that it was John whom Jesus sent to make the preparations for Jesus' final Passover? And it was John whom Jesus wanted nearby during the most vulnerable moment of His life—in the garden—when He prayed and as He wept. It was John who was there to console Him.

And it was John—yes, lying beside Jesus in the upper room—who, when the disciples were confused and didn't know what Jesus was telling them . . . it was John who asked Jesus that tough question no one else dared ask:

"Lord, which one of us is going to betray you? Is it me? It's not me, is it?" (see John 13:25; Matthew 26:22).

They all wanted to know, but it wasn't Peter who asked the question. Peter's the one who asked John to ask the question. Yeah, Peter comes on like horseradish. He loves to trash-talk and jab people with subtle put-downs and sarcastic humor. But here

I think Peter was scared. So scared that he asked sensitive John—supposedly weak, not at all like the "real men" on the team, yet the only one willing to ask what no one else could ask.

Need more?

John was the last one still standing at the cross when all the others (including Peter) had slipped into the shadows.

John was also the only one of Jesus' tribe who had proved loyal enough to care for Jesus' own mother. From the cross He said, "Dear woman, here is your son" (John 19:26).

On resurrection morning, John was the first to arrive at the tomb . . . and the first to fully believe (John 20:3-8).

Later, when Peter and John were hauled before the judicial authorities and instructed to never again preach the name of Jesus, John could say with confidence, "We have to obey God, not man" (Acts 4:19).

So strong was this man of love that tradition claims that when his enemies tried to kill him by boiling him in a cauldron of hot oil, he survived even that! So what do you do with a guy who can survive boiling oil? They stuck him on an island called Patmos, yet even in exile John would not be silenced. See, Jesus chose John (sensitive, emotional, and abundantly strong John) to record, in the book of Revelation, what it's going to be like when Jesus visits us next time.

I don't know what *you* call that kind of strength, but I see in John all that is right about being a man. Jesus said, "Come, follow," so he did. Then Jesus said, "Go fish," and he did.

And isn't it funny that the last guy you'd ever think of as a manly man was the last one standing when the final chapter needed to be written?

CHAPTER 10

TRADING VIOLENCE
FOR VICTORY

I'M NOT SURE WHY, but I've been reflecting the last few days on a couple of very notorious stories. These stories share several striking parallels, but even more surprising, an identical and entirely unexpected conclusion. In fact, these two stories share a finale so breathtaking people are still buzzing about them.

One story took place in March 2005 in Atlanta. The other happened in AD 34 just outside Damascus.

In Atlanta, the main character overpowered a sheriff's deputy, stole her firearm, and shot three people as he made his escape.

Outside Damascus, the main character in this story also presided over another man's death; and, armed with letters further empowering his murderous intentions, he eagerly expanded his rampage.

In Atlanta, the shooter was the target of a twenty-six-hour manhunt, and anyone in his way was a potential target of his rage.

Outside Damascus, this avenger launched his own manhunt, and anyone in "the Way" (see Acts 9:2) was in grave danger.

In Atlanta, the escapee initiated an encounter with a would-be hostage—an encounter that would forever change his life.

Outside Damascus, the target of this murderer's intent actually initiated an encounter with *him*—one that forever changed his life, too.

In Atlanta, the captor immobilized his hostage with masking tape and an extension cord.

Outside Damascus, the would-be hostage immobilized the terrorist with a bright light and a voice from Heaven.

In Atlanta, the resulting encounter included reading from a best-selling Christian book and talking about the Bible.

A description of the encounter outside Damascus is actually included *in* the Bible.

In Atlanta, the killer talked about God.

Outside Damascus, the killer talked *to* God.

In Atlanta, Ashley Smith didn't recognize Brian Nichols until he took off his hat.

Outside Damascus, Saul of Tarsus didn't recognize Jesus of Nazareth until he lost his sight.

In Atlanta, the would-be hostage flipped through her family photo album and asked Nichols to end her family's persecution.

Outside Damascus, Jesus also wanted an end to persecution. "Saul, Saul, why do you persecute me?" (Acts 9:4).

In Atlanta, suggesting that God had a greater purpose for his life, Ashley told Nichols that he had picked her apartment "for a reason."

Outside Damascus, Jesus also had a greater purpose in mind for Saul: "Now get up and go into the city, and you will be told what you must do" (v. 6).

In Atlanta, Brian Nichols called Ashley his "angel sent from God."

Outside Damascus, Saul quickly realized that his visitor *was* God.

And do you want to talk about a dramatic climax? In both stories, folks, in both Atlanta and outside Damascus, a violent, murderous rampage was brought to a peaceful end. In both cases, the would-be assassins waved a white flag and freely surrendered—one to the authorities, the other to his Lord.[1]

BRIAN OF ATLANTA . . . SAUL OF TARSUS

One of the reasons I find the weaving of those stories so intriguing is that prior to each man's encounter you couldn't find two more opposing backgrounds.

Brian Nichols, the suspect accused in the Atlanta courthouse shootings, has been in and out of trouble with the law since his college days. The former Catholic schoolboy turned college athlete turned BMW-driving computer professional had brushes with the law that included everything from disorderly conduct to felony drug use to rape. He cut such a menacing figure that neighbors would avoid eye contact or even stay indoors whenever Brian was around. One neighbor, Gwyn Ring, said, "I tried to avoid being anywhere near him." And she added, "This is not someone I would bake brownies for."[2]

Saul of Tarsus, on the other hand, was a real up-and-comer— a man so gifted and so intelligent and so charismatic that he quickly climbed both the theological *and* political ladders of his day. Even as a young man, he was so fierce in his commitment to God that he was hailed a "Pharisee among Pharisees" and was being groomed for a seat on the Jewish Supreme Court.

But when he heard Peter deliver that impassioned speech before the Sanhedrin (see Acts 5:29-32), and as he listened while Peter described Jesus as having been raised from the dead and now exalted to the right hand of God, and when Peter declared that Jesus was now offering forgiveness of sin to Israel—well, that was more than Saul could take! The hair on the back of his neck leaped to attention, and Saul—well-intentioned, passionately religious, thoroughly moral Saul—decided, "I've got to put a stop to this! Even if I have to kill every last Christ-follower, I'll do it! I will not rest until every single one of them is just like their leader, dangling from a tree."

And that's why, in Acts 8:1, he watched in approval as Stephen was stoned to death. And why, the Bible says in verse 3, he "began to destroy the church. Going from house to house, he dragged off men and women and put them in prison."

His thirst for bloodshed still not quenched, Saul "was still breathing out murderous threats against the Lord's disciples" (9:1). Which is why he asked "for letters to the synagogues in Damascus, so that if he found any there who belonged to the Way, whether men or women, he might take them as prisoners to Jerusalem" (v. 2).

SAUL'S ENCOUNTER

And it was while on his way to do exactly that, that the Lord Jesus Christ initiated a most dramatic encounter. I mean, this encounter had everything—a bright light, a commanding voice, and a divine visitation right there on that dusty, Damascus road. Do you see it?

"As he neared Damascus on his journey, suddenly a light from heaven flashed around him" (v. 3). A light so bright that verse 8 says he was made blind. No doubt dazed and very confused, in shock Saul falls to the ground and stays there—for the first time in his life no longer in control. He just lies there, helpless . . . afraid, as a voice calls out, "Saul, Saul, why do you persecute me?" (v. 4).

Saul wanted to know who was speaking to him.

"I am Jesus, whom you are persecuting," the Lord replied (v. 5).

We're not told this, but I imagine at this moment a deafening silence. Perhaps it lasted only a couple of seconds, but for Saul this was the pause that transformed his life. Because this is the moment he realized, *Jesus isn't dead, is He? I really thought He was! I thought He was a charlatan! A false prophet—and that His followers were doing all these miracles through the power of Satan! I was just trying to defend the faith—but I was wrong, wasn't I? I've never been wrong before; I don't know what to do with this.*

No worries, mate. Jesus is about to tell you what to do with this. "Now get up and go into the city, and you will be told what you must do" (v. 6).

ANOTHER ENCOUNTER

Meanwhile, up ahead in Damascus, the Lord was making another appearance. This time to a nondescript, run-of-the-mill believer named Ananias. Not a power broker by any stretch, just a faithful servant of God doing his part.

But the Lord came to him in a vision and said, "Go to the house of Judas on Straight Street and ask for a man from Tarsus named Saul, for he is praying. In a vision he has seen a man named Ananias come and place his hands on him to restore his sight" (vv. 11, 12).

Now I find it intriguing that Ananias, unlike Saul, is almost argumentative. Saul could barely speak, much less engage the Lord in debate. But Ananias was thinking, *Lord, did you say Saul? I think you said Saul. And if you did say Saul? Uh-uh!* So Ananias said, "I have heard many reports about this man and all the harm he has done to your saints in Jerusalem. And he has come here with authority from the chief priests to arrest all who call on your name" (vv. 13, 14).

Now you understand where he's coming from, don't you? I mean, it's one thing when someone slithers up from behind you in the middle of the night and sticks a gun in your ribs. You don't have any choice but to engage the moment. But when you're asked to knowingly walk right into the teeth of danger? "I don't think so, Lord!"

Back in 1916, Georgia Tech University played a football game against Cumberland University, a tiny regional law school. The Tech team was an overwhelming powerhouse, and they totally dismantled Cumberland by a score of 222 to 0. Needless to say, Tech had also pretty much beat those poor Cumberland players to a pulp.

Near the end of the game, Cumberland's quarterback, Ed Edwards, fumbled a snap from center. As the Tech linemen charged after the ball, Edwards yelled, "Pick it up! Somebody pick it up!" But his fullback, seeing those familiar faces that had hammered him all day, yelled back, "Pick it up yourself—you dropped it."[3]

That's kind of the same spirit I hear in Ananias.

"You want to get this job done? Then *You* pick up the ball, Lord. I mean, if all it took was a bright light to get Saul's attention in the first place, why not use another one? Besides, if a bush worked for Moses, why not try one of those? Or what about a live coal like with Isaiah? That was a pretty cool trick. Do that, Lord! I'll even fire up the grill! I'd even opt for another talking donkey . . . but, Lord! Don't ask *me* to go see Saul!"

Do you know why scaredy-cat Ananias was so forward when bold Saul could barely speak? Because Ananias had a relationship with the Lord, that's why. He knew the Lord's heart and had already come to know that he could trust God with anything. He could bring any burden, any heartache, any temptation—anything before Him. He had confidence whenever he approached the throne (see Hebrews 4:15, 16).

The problem is, Ananias was confidently wrong. This was his divine assignment, folks. This was his calling. He was born to be used for this moment and then to ride into the sunset never to be heard from again.

I say that because in no uncertain terms the Lord said, "Go! This man is my chosen instrument to carry my name before the Gentiles. . . . I will show him how much he must suffer for my name" (Acts 9:15, 16).

So Ananias "went to the house and entered it. Placing his hands on Saul, he said, 'Brother Saul, the Lord—Jesus, who appeared to you on the road as you were coming here—has sent me so that you may see again and be filled with the Holy Spirit.' Immediately, something like scales fell from Saul's eyes, and he could see again. He got up and was baptized" (vv. 17, 18).

DID IT TAKE?

Wow! Is that cool or what? But hang on . . . did it take? I'm serious. Did Saul's life actually change because of this encounter? See, that's what many of us wonder about Brian Nichols. I mean, he said some good stuff, he called Ashley his sister in Christ, and said that before he met her he had been lost. Ashley later said, "I told him I was a child of God and that I wanted to do God's will." Then she said, "And I think he began to want to, too."

But will it take? We don't know yet. We pray it will! But it's safe to say that sometimes it takes time before you can know. Sometimes it takes time to see the fruit of a person's changed life.

That certainly was the case with Saul.

Not that he would have agreed with that assessment. I mean, his hair is still wet from baptism when he grabs a sandwich and then heads right for the synagogue. And what did he do there? He "[preached] . . . that Jesus is the Son of God" (v. 20).

And the Bible says "those who heard him were astonished" (v. 21) but not very trusting. They said, "Isn't he the man who raised havoc in Jerusalem among those who call on this name? And hasn't he come here to take them as prisoners to the chief priests?" (v. 21).

"Sorry, Saul, but I don't think so!" I mean, talk about a flop on your very first preaching gig! Saul laid an egg, folks!

REGROUPING IN ARABIA

Now between verses 21 and 22 there's a huge stretch of time. I know it doesn't read like it—it reads as if verse 22 happened the next day. But it didn't.

What happened is: After his very mediocre reception in Damascus, Saul, wanting to put this whole encounter into some sort of context, went to Arabia and stayed there for three years (see Galatians 1:17). He took his scrolls with him . . . and got this whole deal settled in his heart—you know, the truth about the true nature of Jesus, who He was and what He did. Saul got all that sorted out. He took the time to develop a solid theology of the person and work of Christ. That's when, back to Acts 9, having studied the Scripture and, therefore, having grown powerful in his presentation, Saul returned to Damascus and "baffled the Jews . . . by proving that Jesus is the Christ" (v. 22).

Earlier, verse 20, he had preached Jesus. Now, verse 22—three full years later? He's *proving* Jesus!

The only trouble is, it still wasn't "time." And so, even though Saul had a better message now, the reception from those who heard him was pretty much the same as before. Do you see it? "The Jews conspired to kill him" (v. 23).

And those precious few who did see promise in Saul? They lowered him in a basket through an opening in the wall . . . and Saul got out of Dodge, folks.

That's when he came to Jerusalem. "Surely things will go better for me here! They respect Bible knowledge in Jerusalem!" But, sad to say, "the disciples . . . were all afraid of him, not believing that he really was a disciple" (v. 26).

And even though Barnabas vouched for the guy, the more Saul preached and the more he debated his case, the more those who heard him . . . here we go again . . . "tried to kill him" (v. 29).

That's when the Lord spoke to him in a vision, saying, "I will send you far away to the Gentiles" (22:21). And sure enough, a few of the brothers shipped Saul back to Tarsus.

A TIME OF PEACE

How can you not love Acts 9:31? As soon as Saul was sent away— look at this: "The church throughout Judea, Galilee and Samaria enjoyed a time of peace."

I bet they did! And I think I know why. Even though Saul had all the right information, he was so obnoxious—so in-your-face, so cocksure of the truth of his message—he offended people! He didn't reach people; he ticked 'em off! He probably convinced a lot of folks that he was right, but he also convinced them that he was a jerk! No wonder they wanted to kill him!

Do you understand? Some believers are so committed to being right, that even though they may *be* right, you just want to slug 'em! Get that smirk off your face, Saul! Stop acting like you're so smart! The only reason you know what you know is because God reached down and slapped you around! Remember? Bright light, big voice, face in the dirt?

Besides, Saul, have you stopped to consider the fact that you're obviously not very effective at what you do? I mean, really! Do you see all the corpses lying around, pal? And there aren't that many baptisms to report either . . . are there?

Well, Saul had ten years to think that through. Because that's how long he hung out in obscurity. And during that long decade of waiting (you've heard that word in this book before), God mellows Saul out. It's in obscurity that Saul learns humility and grace and speaking the truth in love. He learns just enough, folks, to realize he doesn't know much.

And it's about then . . . finally . . . that Saul resurfaces as the apostle Paul, and we finally get the sense that, yeah, his Damascus road conversion really did take place after all!

MAKING IT HAPPEN IN PHILIPPI

Now an apostle for Christ, Paul really starts to make tracks. After rehearsing a few of his travels in the opening verses of Acts 16, verse 5 tells us that as a result of Paul's ministry, "the churches were strengthened in the faith and grew daily in numbers."

Aah, that's more like it!

And yet, there was still a governor on him, wasn't there? There was still something holding Paul back.

"Paul and his companions traveled throughout the region of Phrygia and Galatia, having been kept by the Holy Spirit from preaching the word in the province of Asia. When they came to the border of Mysia, they tried to enter Bithynia, but the Spirit of Jesus would not allow them to. So they passed by Mysia and went down to Troas" (vv. 6-8). Please read maturity and humility into that phrase "so they passed by." Because that's what those years in obscurity had cultivated. Paul has actually learned to listen. "During the night Paul had a vision of a man of Macedonia standing and begging him, 'Come over to Macedonia and help us.' After Paul had seen the vision, we got ready at once to leave for Macedonia, concluding that God had called us to preach the gospel to them" (vv. 9, 10).

You see, it wasn't just a matter of time; this waiting period had also been about location. See, God knew exactly where Paul should be preaching. He wanted Paul preaching in Gentile territory.

So, humbly following the Lord's lead, Paul landed in Macedonia, in a bustling seaport city called Philippi. He didn't know why he was in Philippi, but by this point in Paul's walk with God, he didn't need to know why! He was perfectly content with simply following God!

And I'm convinced that as he hit the city limits, Paul just knew that this was where it was all going to come together, baby! Exactly how it would fall, however, no one could have predicted.

He wound up on, of all places, a river bank. And he probably sat there for a while, wondering if maybe this "leading" he had felt was really just a bad pizza. I mean, *Did God actually lead me to do this, or did I just conjure this up all by myself?*

HIS FIRST CONVERT

But then he noticed a group of ladies who were praying. One in particular—Lydia was her name—was a very successful, well-traveled businesswoman. Acts 16 says she was a worshiper of God. And Paul, sensing God's direction, struck up a conversation with her. "The Lord opened her heart" and she responded to Paul's message (v. 14). I take it she'd already been searching, and Paul came along right on cue as God's final piece in the puzzle of her conversion.

We're told that Lydia confessed Christ along with several family members, and that very day she and her entire household were baptized! Right in that same river where these two had met!

Lydia was so overjoyed by her newfound faith that she said to Paul, "You guys got a place to stay?"

"Naw, we figured we'd just pitch a tent over at the KOA."

"Well, I'll have none of that! You're going to stay with me!"

Now that's not bad! Your first convert, plus a parsonage on your first day on the job?! Wow! Paul, no doubt, was thinking, *Way to go, God! This Philippi gig is goin' good! Goooood.*

But hang on: do you remember what the Lord said to Ananias about how Paul would have to "suffer for my name" (9:16)? In other words, Paul wasn't just called to preach; he was called to know pain. Remember that? Well, his suffering wasn't over just because Paul was finally making an impact! In fact, maybe that's why the suffering never *did* leave that man . . . because he *was* making such an impact!

AN UNWANTED ENDORSEMENT

Paul starts moving through the city, leading a whole bunch of people to Christ—but there's this demon-possessed girl who keeps following him! All day every day, she screams at the top of her lungs: "These men are servants of the Most High God, who are telling you the way to be saved!" (16:17).

That's not exactly the kind of endorsement Paul might have hoped for! That would be like Brian Nichols getting busted and the camera zooming in on his polo shirt—and there's the logo of my church! And then he looks into the camera and says, "I'd like to thank my pastor, Steve Wyatt, for all the help he's given me in my walk with Christ!" I mean, thanks but no thanks! That's like Chris Farley doing an ad for Slim·Fast or Richard Simmons endorsing Red Man chewing tobacco. It just doesn't fit!

But this went on for days till, finally, Paul had enough. He spun on his heels and said to that demon, "'In the name of Jesus Christ I command you to come out of her!' At that moment the spirit left her" (v. 18).

Which was good news for the girl, but bad news for her owners. See, she'd made a lot of money for those characters. But when the demon left, so did her psychic power—and their little oil well started spittin' dust!

Totally enraged, the girl's owners dragged Paul before the public officials and falsified some trumped-up charge about disturbing the peace and mocking their sacred religions. The officials believed those charges. Paul and Silas, his traveling companion, were stripped naked and beaten and then thrown into a rat-infested dungeon. Their feet were locked in wooden stocks and their hands put in chains.

And I can't help but wonder if Paul did another gut check as the heavy iron door was slammed shut: *Did God really lead me to come here? I mean, I had a really cool first day, but it's kind of been downhill ever since! And even more, did that Damascus deal really happen? Or did I misread something?*

Now . . . I don't know that he doubted. I know *I* would have. But folks, even if he did? He didn't wallow in that mess very long.

Because the truth is—his baptism *did* take! It's true! Paul had changed more than just his name—Paul was a changed man! A thoroughly devoted follower of Jesus. An apostle of Christ. A vigorous defender of the faith! And he knew that, even in the slammer, God was still God—and his life was in God's hands!

Instead of lying in the refuse of that rat-infested prison, stewing in self-pity, and questioning God's sovereignty, Paul decided to practice what he preached. I mean, here he was, feet locked in wooden stocks, hands shackled with iron chains, and yet Paul decided—can you believe it?—Paul decided to sing!

In the damp, dark misery of a prison cell with their lives hanging in the balance—and no hope they'd ever be set free or even see the dawn of another day—Paul and Silas started singing praise songs. They prayed and they praised. They praised and they prayed. And then they praised some more!

Now folks, that's one way you can know when someone has encountered the real deal. It's because they smile . . . anyway. It's because, even knee-deep in heartache, they're still somehow able to say to God and anyone else who will listen, "I don't know what God is up to, but in the middle of my pain—in the very epicenter of my heartbreak—I'm going to trust Him! So give me a C, Silas! A bouncy C! 'Our God is an awesome God . . .'"

You see, having experienced all those years of obscurity and having tasted what it's like to finally make an impact, Paul saw this prison cell not as confinement but as an opportunity! He viewed his fellow prisoners as a captive audience and his hard-hearted warden as yet another soul for whom Christ died.

And so . . . he sings! He sings and sings and sings!

And the Lord God so loved what He heard that when His voice rumbled out a hearty "AMEN!" His pleasure in their praise literally brought the house down! I mean, talk about rock 'n' roll, baby! Chains snapped, doors flung open, prison walls crumbled to the ground. I imagine that God was saying, "I like that. I like it when my children suffer with grace!"

What happened was that an earthquake struck right along the fault line of that prison. And those two prisoners and all the others were suddenly free to make a run for it!

But they didn't.

The jailer thought they had, so he drew his sword, prepared to do what his superiors were going to do to him anyway. But before he could, Paul called out, "Surprise!" Well, not exactly . . . but close. And the jailer, so stunned that they'd actually stuck around—and because he had already eavesdropped on their marathon songfest—asked Paul to tell him about his God. Trust me, it wasn't Paul's singing that reached him. It was *that* he sang, that's what grabbed him. And so the jailer asked, "What must I do to be saved?" (v. 30).

Paul replied, "Believe in the Lord Jesus, and you will be saved" (v. 31).

And so he did. Then, overwhelmed with joy, he pleaded with Paul and Silas to come to his home and explain the gospel to his family. And they believed, too! And then, lo and behold, they tip-toed out to the river and had another baptism service—that very night!

Toward daybreak, the jailer started getting antsy. I imagine he said something like, "Would you fellas mind coming back to prison? Because if my boss clocks in and you're not there, I'm dead!" So they went back, and the next morning when the officials discovered that Paul had been improperly arrested—because he, in fact, was a Roman citizen—they released him with the understanding (and I love this) that he leave their city and never return.

Isn't that so typical for Paul? The dude's still getting kicked out of town, but at least now it's because he's making an impact! His life is makin' a difference!

Did that Damascus road encounter "take"? You bet it did. You bet your life it did!

TWO ENCOURAGING TAKEAWAYS

I have two takeaways from this story—takeaways that I firmly believe will encourage a whole lot of people, maybe even you.

You can't trump God's mercy. That's the first. It doesn't matter how far you have fallen, no one has ever sunk beneath the reach of God. Because the same God who visited a mass murderer just outside Damascus is also the same God who sent an "angel" to a murderer in Atlanta.

Why does God initiate such audacious, inexplicable encounters? Because grace is the great hope of the Christian message, that's why. There is no amount or depth of sin that could ever trump God's mercy. There is no act so heinous that would ever cause God to give up on you. The Bible says, "where sin increase[s], grace increase[s] all the more" (Romans 5:20).

So don't sit there and tell me—or even more, tell God—that you're too far gone. That your past is so soiled, life for you could never be any different than it is right now.

That's a lie! It comes straight from the pit of Hell, so don't you dare believe it! There is not one person on this planet—not Brian Nichols, not Scott Peterson, not even Osama bin Laden—who has so thoroughly blown it that God, in His mercy, cannot forgive!

I mean, it's just what God does. He loves to take all of our rusted-out failures—our mangled excuse of a life—and He loves to reshape and remold us into shiny, glistening trophies to His amazing grace.

And if you haven't had an encounter with that grace? Listen, it's never too late to get started. Whatever you have done, whatever you may have become, it doesn't matter. What you need to do is what Paul did. You need to "humble yoursel[f] before the Lord, and he will lift you up" (James 4:10).

He will. He really will.

God always finishes what He starts. The second takeaway is for those who have already had an encounter. What you need to take from this story is this: It doesn't matter how far you are from where you need to be. Whatever work God started in you, He will complete it.

That truth comes from the very pen of Paul himself. See, several years after this prison experience, Paul got tossed into yet another prison. (Isn't it funny how he launched his career tossing Christians in the slammer and yet wound up spending so much time there himself?)

It was during this second hitch in the slammer that Paul writes his old friends in Philippi, many of whom had found Christ under his teaching. So Paul writes them a letter of encouragement. And even though he's writing it from prison—the theme of the letter is joy!

A joy that knows more than its share of scars.

A contentment that is unapologetically sourced in pain.

A sense of purpose that will *not* be diluted by hardship or suffering.

We're talking, folks, the kind of joy that set Paul to singing that dark, lonely midnight so many years before.

And now, all these years later, in a letter to his friends, Paul shares an amazing truth. In those early days, when no one would believe him and everyone refused to listen to him—when his life held no meaning, his past having been stripped away and his future so very much in doubt—it was this truth that became Paul's anchor.

I'm sure he struggled to believe it as he was lowered in a basket over the Damascus wall or ushered out of Jerusalem. It was a lesson he longed to believe—but how could he believe it?—first in Arabia and then later during that decade of obscurity.

But the melody in his heart would not be silenced. So once again, in yet another musty prison cell, did Paul start humming as he wrote these wonderful words of truth: "He who began a good work in you will [bring it] to completion" (Philippians 1:6).

Now whether those words began as melody or prose to lift his own heart, when Paul included those lines in his letter, God preserved that song for you and me.

> *He who began a good work in you,*
> *He who began a good work in you,*
> *will be faithful to complete it,*
> *He'll be faithful to complete it;*
> *He who started the work*
> *will be faithful to complete it in you.*[4]

This isn't just Paul's truth; it's your truth, too. You mark it down and you mark it well: if God has begun His good work in your life, He will complete it. He will!

Whether your starting place was a dramatic light from Heaven or a prison-crumbling earthquake . . . whether it was more akin to a private discussion of *The Purpose-Driven Life* over pancakes or a reflective afternoon chat beside a strong-flowing river . . .

Whatever your point of beginning, if you can point back to some time in your life when you had an encounter with God, some moment when you bowed before the cross of Christ and offered Him your life . . .

Then trust Him when He says it: He who began that work is just as committed to completing that work.

Please . . . hear from God right now. If your faith had a starting place, that same faith will carry you all the way home. God will see to it.

Even if you feel as though your encounter might not have taken. Even if you're right that you're so far from where you need to be.

So sing! Come on! Just sing . . . anyway.

PART THREE

The cross He occupied had your name on it. His crown of thorns had been fitted for you. The pain and anguish He endured, you deserved. The abuse and slander and devastation He experienced . . . was intended for you.

But instead, "by his wounds you have been healed" (1 Peter 2:24).

CHAPTER 11

THE GREATEST TRADE OF ALL

BEFORE YOU READ another word, I want you to pause and take a long and studied mental look at your Savior. I want you to do that because the writer of the book of Hebrews said we should do that. He said, "Let us fix our eyes on Jesus . . . who . . . endured the cross, scorning its shame" (12:2).

So do it.

Fix your eyes on Jesus.

Picture Him in all of His agony and distress.

Picture the nails . . . and the angry crowd.

Picture the spit in His face and the blood trickling down His brow.

Go ahead, form in your mind that all-compelling image.

Now . . . ask yourself this: why did He do it? Why did He so willingly endure all that abuse?

Two reasons: respect for His Father and compassion for you and me. Make no mistake, friend, Jesus' death was directed by the Father, but it was driven by His love. He died so that we could live. He was wounded that I might be healed.

Do you see the verse? "He himself bore our sins in his body on the tree, so that we might die to sins and live for righteousness; by his wounds you have been healed" (1 Peter 2:24).

You just can't escape it, no matter how you try. Jesus hung on that cross . . . for you. He was despised and rejected, beaten and mocked, flogged and crucified—for you.

The cross He occupied had your name on it. His crown of thorns had been fitted for you. The pain and anguish He endured, you deserved. The abuse and slander and devastation He experienced . . . was intended for you.

But instead, "by his wounds you have been healed."

The phrase "by his wounds" is written in the original in the singular, not plural. We can read it "by his wound." Why? Jesus' unfair treatment was so awful that not even *The Passion of the Christ* could fully capture its horror. Could it be that Jesus was so mangled and so mistreated that He didn't have "wounds" so much as His body was just one long, unbroken wound? Isaiah said His appearance "was so disfigured beyond that of any man and his form marred beyond human likeness" that . . . get this: "many . . . were appalled at him" (Isaiah 52:14).

And it was by the one long, unbroken wound, Peter tell us, that you (make note of that), YOU have been healed.

Talk about Trading Places! Folks, the cross is, without question, the greatest trade in the history of the world! Far more significant than Schilling to the Red Sox. Far more earth-shattering than the Babe to the Yankees is that the cross that was intended for me was shouldered, instead, by Him.

And when He died—as He breathed His last—all earth was so confused by what was such an obviously senseless loss that nature itself convulsed: the ground shook like an earthquake, tombs cracked open, the solar system shuddered, the sun hid, and the sky went black!

But why? Why the shock? Why the surprise? Listen, from the beginning of time God had promised a solution to man's deepest problem. And now, finally, at history's perfect moment, the Lamb of God had come. And He shed His blood, laying down His life for our sin that we might be healed. I mean, isn't that what He was supposed to do?

THE CROSS . . . NOT JUST A BAD DAY

Of course it was! Listen, as bad as it got on Calvary—and it got really, really bad—the cross was not an accident; it was Jesus' ultimate assignment.

Peter said that Jesus "was handed over . . . by God's set purpose and foreknowledge" (Acts 2:23). The cross was neither a bad day nor a tragic surprise. It was God's plan. His predetermined decision. Isaiah said, "It was the LORD's will to crush him" (Isaiah 53:10).

So unwavering was God's plan that Jesus actually planted the tree from which the beams of His cross were carved. He placed into the earth's belly the very ore that was used to cast the nails that held His hands in place. Jesus, the Lamb, knew of His death and His destiny before the world was created and before He took His first breath!

That's why He rebuked Peter for slicing off the guy's ear. That's why Pilate didn't intimidate Him. That's why the ropes that cuffed His wrists weren't even necessary. That's why no guards were needed to keep Him on the tree. He wasn't going anywhere! He had an appointment to keep! And even if there had been no Judas, no trial, no soldiers, and no Pilate—Jesus would have climbed that hill and nailed himself to that tree if He had to! Because He was God's Lamb!

Some people think of the cross as sort of an ancient version of *Harold and the Purple Crayon*. Have you ever read that book? It's a children's book I used a lot during my consulting days. The plot is really simple: a little bald-headed kid with a big purple crayon keeps drawing himself into and out of various situations. For example, if he's on a path that's way too long, he just draws himself a shortcut. If he's hungry, he draws a couple of pies. If he finds himself in deep water, he just draws a boat! If he's lonely, he draws a friend.

Now I used to use that book as a motivator to help planning teams find creative solutions to what otherwise appeared to be unsolvable problems. I'd tell them Harold's story and then encourage them to just take out their crayons and draw their way through, too.

But God is not Harold, and He didn't draw up the redemption of mankind on the fly. We tend to think He did! The world got all messed up, and God—not knowing quite what to do—grabbed a crayon and drew a cross.

But that's not how it happened. The cross was no tragic surprise. Calvary was not some knee-jerk response to a world plummeting toward destruction. It wasn't a patch job or some stopgap measure. The truth is, the cross was always God's plan. A pre-creation decision. Remember? "It was the Lord's will to crush him" (Isaiah 53:10).

Which means what? It was God's will that there would be bloodshed. It was His plan all along! So don't blame Mel Gibson for all the gore. That decision came from several levels above even his pay grade.

Now I understand if this whole blood thing disturbs you. But you need to know that from the beginning of time, God ordained that blood would be *the* key component—the hyperlink, if you will—connecting us with His forgiveness.

In fact, that's the first of five rules relating to blood that you need to come to grips with if you're ever going to know the healing that God longs to provide.

Blood Is Required to Cover Sin

Rule #1: Blood is required to cover sin. Tucked away in the constitution of ancient Israel, in the book of Leviticus, are God's words,
"For the life of a creature is in the blood, and I have given it to
you to make atonement for yourselves on the altar; it is the blood
that makes atonement for one's life" (Leviticus 17:11).

In other words, it is *blood* that God chose as the reconciling
agent—the cleansing, covering connection—that would deliver
to us the forgiveness of sin. In fact, the Bible says, "without the
shedding of blood there is no forgiveness" (Hebrews 9:22).

Now you may not like that. I'm not so sure I like it, either. But
guess what? This is God's world, and He has the right to set it up
however He chooses. So just chill out . . . and when you get around
to creating *your* own universe? Set it up any way you like. But this
is *God's* world so you've got to play by His rules. And Rule #1 says,
"If you want to be saved, it's going to take some blood."

The Blood of a Substitute

But not just any blood. God's Rule #2 is that this blood must be the
blood of a substitute. The price for forgiveness, God decided—not
me, God—would have to be paid by someone other than you.
Now this "substitute blood" actually finds its genesis in Genesis—in the garden, when Adam and Eve first sinned. As soon as
they ate the fruit, the Bible says, their eyes were opened and they
knew that they were naked (see Genesis 3:7). I take it that up till
then, they hadn't even noticed! But now, not only did they notice,
they felt shame! So they tried to cover themselves with fig leaves,
but you know how leaves are. They tear up and dry out and wilt
and crumble—I mean, leaves are a wardrobe malfunction just
waitin' to happen! So what did God do? He "made garments of
skin" (v. 21) for them.

How do you get skin from an animal? You kill it, right? You slaughter it and then you skin it.

Can you imagine Adam's horror as he watched God take a poor, defenseless little creature and strike it down and then tear away its flesh? You've got to know he was thinking, *Why did we eat that fruit? We weren't supposed to. God said not to. And now look at all the suffering we've caused!*

Then there was the time on Mount Moriah, when God commanded Abraham to take his only son and lay him on an altar, then raise a knife and kill him. Isaac was confused. As they climbed the mountain of sacrifice, he said, "Dad, we got the wood, we got the fire . . . but where's the lamb?" With great emotion, Abraham said, "God himself will provide the lamb . . . , my son" (Genesis 22:8).

You may know the rest of the story. Abraham tied Isaac to the altar, then raised his knife into the air, fully prepared to thrust it into his dear son's heart—when suddenly an angel called out, "Abraham!" Abraham probably thought, *I am so glad you called!* And when Abraham looked up, "there in a thicket he saw a ram caught by its horns. He went over and took the ram and sacrificed it . . . instead of his son" (v. 13).

Abraham didn't know it at the time, but that heart-stopping experience was a foreshadowing of God's intent to provide an even greater substitute! Another "only Son" who, on this future occasion, would not be spared—but who, as the precious Lamb of God, would be offered by God as the full and complete blood payment for all the sins of all the world.

A Substitute Without Blemish

Rule #3 builds on Rule #2 by adding this wrinkle: The substitute must be without blemish. The explanation is found in Exodus 12, at the end of the account of the ten plagues. Pharaoh, to date, had stubbornly refused to release the Israelites from captivity. Even after nine horrible plagues, he still refused to budge. But the tenth and final plague was the worst of all: if Pharaoh still refused, the death angel would pass over Egypt and every firstborn son in the land would die, while the firstborn children of the Israelites would survive. How would the angel know which homes were Jewish and which were not?

Well, a lamb was to be chosen for each household—a perfect, blemish-free lamb, one "without defect" (Exodus 12:5). And they were to slaughter the lambs and paint the blood on the doorframes of their homes. That way, when the death angel passed by, seeing the blood on the doorframes, he would *pass over* . . . hence the name Passover.

Once again, blood was the vehicle of salvation!

In the garden, we learned that blood was required to provide covering.

On Mount Moriah, we learned that God would provide a substitute.

And at the Passover, we learned that the lamb had to be without defect. No taint, no blemish was allowed.

Now once the Israelites were free, they traveled to the base of Mount Sinai where they received God's law. And a very central part of that law had to do with sacrifice. See, in God's unfolding plan for forgiveness, we learn, through the law, that the procedure for tapping into His grace required even more bloodshed.

The law stated that whenever sin occurred, the offender was to "bring as his offering a male [animal] without defect" (Leviticus 4:23). Bulls, goats, lambs, doves or pigeons—the animal depended on your position in the community. Where were the animals brought? To the place of worship. Which means, folks, that in the Old Testament whenever you went to church? Everybody would know you had a problem, right? Because you've got this animal tucked under your arm, right?

Now today, we come with our Bibles tucked in that same location! And we all understand the rule: the bigger the Bible, the more h-h-h-h-holy is the one who carries it!

But back then? Well, I picture it like this: the bigger the animal, the more visible your screw-up! "Brother Daniel really messed up this week; look at the size of that beast!"

Finally at the altar, the sinner would "lay his hand" on the animal (v. 24). He would lean his weight on the animal, in effect saying, "I transfer my guilt, my sin, to this lamb."

Personally Applied

Blood is required for covering. It must be the blood of a substitute. A worthy substitute must be without blemish. But then, having selected our substitute, we are to *lean* on that substitute; that is, I must personally appropriate the blood of this animal for *my* sin!

And that's Rule #4 for receiving forgiveness. It's about an amazing transfer. My sin would become that lamb's sin. And with the sacrifice of that animal, I would be forgiven.

Now . . . can you imagine living like that?

Every day, from dawn till dusk, the priests stood at the altar . . . sprinkling blood. Such a scene was so commonplace in those days, historians tell us, that the average person's clothing was permanently blood-stained.

Because day in and day out, week in and week out, year in and year out—Israelites were trudging to the altar with animals under their arms. Because if you sinned you had to find an animal. Then you had to go to the place of worship. Then you had to *lean* on the animal while you slaughtered it and watch while the priest caught the animal's blood and sprinkled that blood on the altar.

And only after all of that were you finally forgiven!

But then you leave church, try to merge onto that glorified parking lot we call I-17, and, totally frustrated, you wave at somebody with a very odd-looking hand gesture! So you've got to turn around, find another lamb, and do the whole deal all over again! Every single day of your life!

A Sacrifice to End All Sacrifices

Which is why Isaiah's words came to mean so much to the Jews. They were so tired of dealing with their sin and so weary from all that bloodshed. So when Isaiah said, "He was pierced for our transgressions, [and] crushed for our iniquities" (Isaiah 53:5), it was like a breath of fresh air! Because these people had been piercing and crushing animals for years! But now, instead of an "it," there would come a "he"!

"We all, like sheep, have gone astray, each of us has turned to his own way; and the LORD has laid on him the iniquity of us all" (v. 6).

Do you see that? "On him." Isaiah, with a hope-filled vision, prophesied a different kind of trade. Instead of trading my sins to an animal, God said that one day He would trade the sins of all mankind—past, present, and future—to the shoulders of a "him"! But this "him," this Lamb, instead of just temporarily covering sin, would remove sin . . . forever! His sacrifice, His blood would provide *permanent* forgiveness. And that's Rule #5: A sacrifice to end all sacrifices would soon be made.

Talk about a wonderful promise! And oh, how the Israelites longed for God's Lamb to just come and put an end to all that bloodshed! But after Isaiah put down his pen, seven hundred years passed—and still no Lamb. Seven hundred years of sacrifice. Seven hundred years of bloodshed! "The blood of bulls and goats" kept flowing even though Scripture says, "it is impossible for [that kind of blood] to take away sins" (Hebrews 10:4). God said, "It has to be HIS blood! The blood of *Him*. I'm going to lay *all* of the iniquity of *all* the world on *Him! And only *His* blood can take that sin away!"

FULFILLED IN CHRIST

Now think back over the five rules I just gave you and keep them in mind, because all five were fulfilled by Christ.

Rule #1

Rule #1, that blood is required to cover sin, would be fulfilled in this coming "Him" Isaiah talked about. Are you following me? *Jesus'* blood would provide my covering . . . and yours, too. Let's check off Rule #1 as already fulfilled.

Rule #2

Sure enough, seven hundred years after Isaiah's prophecy, a stranger appeared in the wilderness. And he was a real freak. I mean, the dude wore camel hair and ate locusts and drank wild honey (Venti, extra whip . . . definitely not decaf). His followers called him the Baptizer, and he traveled the countryside telling all who would listen of a new kingdom. He even prophesied that there was one coming after him who was so great . . . so holy . . . that John wouldn't even be worthy to lace up His Nikes.

And when the great one appeared and John first saw Him, he immediately thought of Isaiah. He cried out, "Look, the Lamb of God, who takes away the sin of the world!" (John 1:29). Could it be? Has He really come? God's intended substitute? The "him" who will put an end to all this sacrificial madness? The fulfillment of God's Rule #2? "Yes!" John is saying. "He's God's Lamb! He has finally come. And He's going to take away *all* sin . . . once and for all!"

Jesus, God's only Son, out of obedience to the Father and love for mankind, willingly emptied himself and became *our* Lamb! But even though everybody had been looking for Him, when He finally came so few seemed to recognize Him. Not even the religious bunch who tried to trip Him up. And when they couldn't trip him up, they determined to tear Him down.

Crowds laughed at Him. Scoffers mocked Him. His detractors ridiculed Him. His own family scorned Him. The soldiers at Pilate's Praetorium taunted Him. They blindfolded and hit Him. He stood naked before them, their spit mixed with His blood streaming down His face.

Then came Calvary.

Jesus carried His own instrument of death up that rugged hillside. His tired, abused body took the form of a cross as nails were driven into His palms, piercing them as the iron gripped deeply into the wood. His cross was then lifted between two thieves and dropped with a thud into its prepared hole.

And for six long hours, our Savior, Jesus, dangled perilously between Heaven and earth. Meanwhile, the disciples cowered in the shadows. One of the thieves crucified alongside Jesus cried out for mercy; the other scoffed in foolish pride.

The leering crowd taunted Jesus, saying, "Come down from the cross! Then we'll believe you, King!" But there was no rescue, no miracle—only a shout of agony that rumbled across the horizon like roaring thunder as Jesus, His body wracked with pain, cried, "My God, why have you forsaken me?" (Mark 15:34). Later He whispered, "It is finished" (John 19:30). And then He died. Check off Rule #2.

Rules #3 and #5

But understand—He *had* to die. Because Jesus, and only Jesus, was qualified! Remember Rule #3? The only blood that would suffice was blood from a Lamb without blemish.

In all of human history, there is only one who has lived without sin. And so only one was qualified to pay the price.

Check off Rule #3. The Bible says, "God made him who had no sin to be sin for us, so that in him we might become the righteousness of God (2 Corinthians 5:21). That's why He had to die! Because He had "no sin." He was "without defect," Peter says. And that's why Paul, in 1 Corinthians 5:7, calls Jesus, "our Passover lamb."

The Bible says, in no uncertain terms, that because Jesus came and because He died, "there is no longer any sacrifice for sin" (Hebrews 10:18). No more lambs are required. No more blood needs to be spilled. All that will ever be needed is already fully supplied. The Bible says, "We have been made holy through the sacrifice of the body of Jesus Christ [*get this*] once for all" (v. 10). So let's check that one off, too, whaddaya say? Rule #5: The sacrifice to end all sacrifice has been made. Not another lamb will be required.

Rule #4

But one rule is not checked off. Do you know what is still needed? Rule #4, right? Because just as with the Jews in the Old Testament, *forgiveness is not supplied until His blood is personally applied.* Just as on that first Passover evening, you've got to take the blood that Jesus freely provided, and if you want forgiveness, you've got to splash His blood across the doorframe of your heart. You've got to lean heavy on the Lamb of God, taking all that you are—all the gunk, all the garbage, all the stinkin', putrid filth you've ever done—and you've got to bundle it up and personally hand it over to Jesus.

If you're not willing to do that? God cannot forgive you. There is no grace, friend; there is no redemption, there is no forgiveness because *there is no other plan.*

When you stand before God on that day of judgment, He's not going to ask about your personal value system or your church attendance or how much money you donated to the tsunami relief. All He's going to want to know is: "What did you do with the blood of the Lamb? The blood that I freely provided for you. Did you apply it to your life? Did you splash it across the door to your heart? Did you rely on that sin offering—and that offering alone—as your only hope for cleansing? Or did you try to sew some leaves together? Did you try to manufacture your own covering? What did you do with the blood?"

Since it's so important that you grasp this teaching, I've put this truth in a visual that I hope will help you fully understand. And what I want you to do is follow the prepositions as I describe them, because those tiny prepositions represent the difference between your being covered or being condemned.

IN sin. The three crosses at right represent Jesus and the two thieves, convicted criminals who were also crucified that day. Now the two thieves were both obviously  "in sin," right? That's why they were hanging there. They were lawbreakers and, therefore, "*in* sin."

NO sin. But Jesus, represented by the middle cross, had "no sin," according to 2 Corinthians 5:21: "God made him who had no sin to be sin for us, so that in him we

might become the righteousness of God." Jesus was without blemish. And we know that because it was His perfect life that qualified Him to shoulder this awesome assignment.

BECAME sin. Once Jesus was on the cross, however, God made Him to "be sin." He had no sin of His own, but because He was willing and because He was qualified, he "became sin." Why?

FOR us. "For us," according to 2 Corinthians 5:21. And that is what we've been calling the Greatest Trade of all. Isaiah said it, too: "We all, like sheep, have gone astray, each of us has turned to his own way; and the LORD has laid on him the iniquity of us all" (Isaiah 53:6). My sin "on him." My cross . . . on His back. My nails . . . in His hands. He died "for us." *All* of us.

ON Him. Read Isaiah 53:6 again. What that means is that all sin—past, present, and future; your sin, my sin, all sin—was laid on Jesus on the cross. Includ-

ing the sin of those who believe and those who don't believe, those who choose to follow and those who stubbornly walk away. *All* means all, and it was all "on Him" as His body hung from that cross.

IN Him. But here's where Rule #4 begins to inject its power. Those who tap into Christ's blood benefit from its life-giving flow. Even though all our iniquity is "on Him," when we

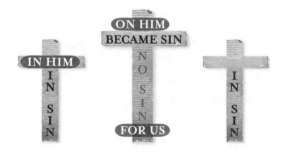

personally appropriate His blood into our lives, we are forgiven. Just like the thief who reached out to Christ. Remember? By faith he tapped in, didn't he? And because he did, he became "in Him." "God made him who had no sin to be sin for us so that *in him* we might become the righteousness of God."

Died TO sin.
And that's exactly what happened to that criminal. By faith he made that very personal appropriation. He splashed the blood

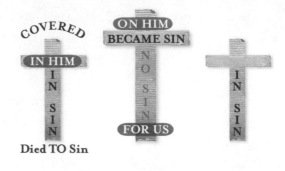

Died TO Sin

of Jesus across his heart, and in doing so, he died—do you see it?—to sin. And in dying to his sin, he died fully covered by Jesus' forgiving blood.

Died IN sin.
The other thief, however, did *not* believe. He scoffed at the thought that blood could forgive. And so, even though all of his iniquities were also "on Him,"

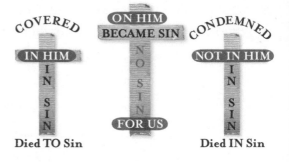

Died TO Sin   Died IN Sin

he refused to make the vital connection. He died still in his sin—and, therefore, he died forever condemned.

Now get this: the only difference between these two men is that one made the connection while the other did not.

I know . . . it's almost incomprehensible, but listen to me: the creator God of the universe has offered to Trade Places with you. In fact, the actual transaction has already been accomplished. He has already been pierced for all your transgressions. He has already been crushed for all your iniquities. Every sin you have ever done—and those you haven't yet done (but will do)—every single one of them has already been placed "on Him."

Christ has already fulfilled four of the five rules God established for receiving forgiveness. And the only rule that remains is the only one that can be accomplished only by you.

You've got to . . .

Complete the Connection

When He was cross, you were on His mind. He saw more than just the destruction of that awful moment—He saw you. He saw you in the vortex of your own heartache. He saw you spinning helplessly in a world gone mad. He saw you battered and beaten by sin. He saw you crushed and defeated. He saw you betrayed by people you love. He saw you alone and afraid. He saw you slopping around in the muck of your own foolish choices. . . .

He saw you there, and He refused to let you stay there. So He marched right into hell itself, so you wouldn't have to.

And that, folks, is the real message of Easter! Because—can you believe it?—the one who died didn't stay dead! Three days later, He walked out of that tomb gloriously and victoriously alive!

But please understand: the truth that gives this truth its amazing, awesome, and world-changing power is that He was the only one qualified to die in the first place. And even though He didn't have to, He chose to.

Jesus Christ left Heaven so you could go to Heaven. And He went through hell so you wouldn't have to. And even though you may have piled up a bazillion dumpsters full of reeking, stinkin' garbage, He traded places with you . . . anyway. And all of that smelly refuse? It's already been recycled—forever filtered—through the blood He so willingly shed on the cross.

Listen, the trade has already been made. The deal is already struck. *All that's left is for you to complete the connection.*

"How do I do that?"

You start by admitting that you need that connection. You admit, first to yourself and then to God, that the blood-stained cross of Jesus is your only hope . . . and your only salvation.

And then, you place your sins where God already put them—"on Him." And then, by faith you come to Him. You tell Him that you want His covering, that you want to be *in* Him. And it doesn't matter how you say it, just use whatever feeble words happen to trickle out. Trust me, He'll understand.

This is the beginning of the Great Exchange. It's a process, to be sure, but the process begins with a simple prayer of childlike submission: "Jesus, I accept you as the Lamb of my life. Take me, Lord. Take the good, the bad, and the ugly. Take every part of who I am. And cover me . . . as only You can do."

A FINAL FOOTNOTE

On the evening after I had completed this last chapter, two of our men—while trying to install a new lighting system that would get some very unsightly light trees out of the view of our projection screens—took a bad tumble.

Thank God, neither was seriously injured, but ever since that night, Trading Places has taken on an even more poignant meaning for me. Because that's all I wanted in those hours immediately following the accident. I played and replayed their fall in my mind, and all I wished for was that it would have been me on that lift instead of them.

TRADING PLACES

I felt so very responsible. After all, it was my desire they were trying to fulfill. The lighting truss was something that I wanted to have done by Easter, and Ron and Marv, amazing servants that they are, were more than willing to make that happen.

So I went there, baby. Guilt Central. These two good men were now suffering . . . for me? Now, I know they were doing it for the Lord—but that's just where my grief took me. And that sense of feeling responsible yet unharmed was almost more than I could bear.

I didn't sleep well that night. In fact, after being startled once again from my sleep by that same recurring image replaying over and over in my brain, I got up and went to my study.

Still wishing that somehow I could have traded places with these men—still bothered by the feeling of being responsible yet unharmed—I started looking through my notes on this chapter.

And there it was. Isaiah 53:6: "We all, like sheep, have gone astray, each of us has turned to his own way; and the LORD has laid on him [*on Him, not on me*] the iniquity of us all." Do you see it?

We're responsible, yet unharmed.

Then I read 2 Corinthians 5:21: "God made him who had no sin to be sin for [me], so that in him [I] might become the righteousness of God."

Once again, I'm responsible . . . yet unharmed.

And then I read 1 Peter 2:24: "He himself bore [my] sins in his body on the tree, so that [I] might die to sins and live for righteousness; by his wounds [I] have been healed."

There it was again: I'm responsible . . . yet unharmed.

And that's when the Father said to me, "Steve, I couldn't bear the image that kept replaying in my mind, either. I kept seeing you wandering and so desperate. I saw the awful brokenness caused by your sin. And I just knew something had to be done."

And that's why, in a trade unlike any other trade in all of human history, God visited earth . . . for one reason:

To wear the crown I was supposed to wear.

To receive the nails I should have received.

To bleed and suffer and die . . . in my place.

I mean, I'm responsible . . . yet unharmed.

Phil Johnson wrote a song with these words:

I'm the one to blame
I caused all His pain
He gave Himself
The day He wore my crown[1]

Jesus gave himself. He released His own blood. He made the trade that would save my life—that day He chose to wear my crown. Precious Jesus, that You would Trade Places with a screw-up like me is beyond my mind to conceive. Knowing what I am and what I've done, yet taking my place—absorbing the punishment I deserved—reflects a love quite unlike any love I've ever known.

And that's why I'm determined to make a change. God, freely renovate my life. Not because I feel so undeniably guilty, but because I feel so unquestionably loved.

Having given You my heart, I'll never trade Your rightful place for any other.

Amen.

N O T E S

CHAPTER 1, THE GREAT EXCHANGE

1. Vicki Michaelis, "Swim star Phelps faces DUI charges" (USA Today, November 9, 2004), Sports Section C.

CHAPTER 2, PUTTING ON AND PUTTING OFF

1. Dan Hamilton, *Forgiveness* (Downers Grove: InterVarsity Press, 1980), 6.

CHAPTER 3, THE *X* FACTOR

1. http://www.jellomuseum.com/#History

CHAPTER 5, TRADING REJECTION FOR ROYALTY

1. Steve Rosenbloom, *The Chicago Tribune,* February 6, 2005.

2. *Fiddler on the Roof* by Joseph Stein opened on Broadway in 1964 with music by Jerry Bock and lyrics by Sheldon Harnick.

3. http://www.benjerry.com/our_company/about_us/our_history/jerrybio.cfm

CHAPTER 6, TRADING WHINING FOR WINNING

1. Ernest Kurtz, *Not-God: A History of Alcoholics Anonymous* (Center City: Hazelden Pittman Archives Press), 35.

2. Phillip Yancey, "Lessons From Rock Bottom," *Christianity Today,* July 11, 2000.

3. Insoo Kim Berg and Scott D. Miller, *Working with the Problem Drinker: A Solution-Focused Approach* (New York: W.W. Norton & Co., 1992), 13.

4. J. Keith Miller, *A Hunger for Healing* (HarperSanFrancisco, 1991), 50-51.

CHAPTER 8, TRADING BEAUTY FOR BRAVERY

1. http://teacherlink.ed.usu.edu/tlresources/units/Byrnes-famous/rubybrid.html

2. http://www.orthodoxytoday.org/articles4/MotherTeresaAbortion.shtml

3. http://www.mecca.org/~crights/dream.html

4. From "The Voices of Indonesia" by Ming Haw Lim, from *The Voice of the Martyrs.*

5. http://smiley963.tripod.com/misc1998.html

6. Max Lucado, *Life Lessons from the Inspired Word of God: Books of Ruth and Esther* (W Publishing Group, 1996) p. 43.

7. Vince Lombardi, Jr., *What It Takes To Be #1: Vince Lombardi on Leadership* (New York: McGraw-Hill, 2001), 46.

8. David Claerbaut, Bart Starr: *When Leadership Mattered* (Dallas: Taylor Trade Publishing, 2004), 224.

9. Steve Strahl, compiler, *365 Daily Success Quotes,* ebook, © Lion Publications, San Marco, TX. http://www.lionpublications.com/download-365.htm

10. Alan Loy McGinnis, *Bringing Out the Best in People: How to Enjoy Helping Others Excel* (Minneapolis: Augsburg Fortress Publishers, 1985), 17-18.

CHAPTER 9, TRADING POTENTIAL FOR PASSION

1. Stephen R. Covey, *The 7 Habits of Highly Effective People* (New York: Simon & Shuster, 1989), 278-279.

2. See John 11:33-38. The Greek term for the words "deeply moved" in vv. 33, 38 has as one of its primary meanings "snort like a horse."

CHAPTER 10, TRADING VIOLENCE FOR VICTORY

1. Compiled from a variety of news reports, including Bpnews.net/bpnews. asp?ID=20340, *The Associated Press* (3/14/2005), and *The Atlanta Journal Constitution.*

2. Audra D.S. Burch, "Neighbors were in fear of suspect," The Miami Herald, March 14, 2005.

3. Fred Russell, *I'll Try Anything Twice* (Nashville: The McQuiddy Press, 1945), 17.

4. "He Who Began a Good Work in You" words and music by Jon Mohr, © 1987 Birdwing Music and Jonathan Mark Music.

CHAPTER 11, THE GREATEST TRADE OF ALL

1. "The Day He Wore My Crown," words and music by Phil Johnson, © 1978 Multisongs, Inc.

Have you made a decision to commit your life to Jesus Christ as a result of reading this book? If you are wondering what to do next, we encourage you to look for a church in your area and ask how new believers are welcomed into the family of God. The following Scriptures may be helpful to you as well:

John 3:16
1 John 1:8
Romans 6:23
Acts 20:21
Acts 4:12
Romans 10:9
Acts 2:38
John 13:35

We welcome your comments and questions. Write to us at:
tradingplaces@standardpub.com

You're not alone when you ask,
Where's God?

And you don't have to be alone in the search for an answer.

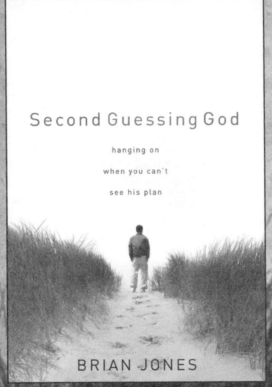

Second Guessing God

hanging on

when you can't

see his plan

BRIAN JONES

0-7847-1841-5

Let Second Guessing God be your personal guide to finding strength
and meaning as you face trouble, pain, loneliness, or doubt.

*Brian Jones . . . expresses the heart's disappointment and longing with a
directness that somehow always ends up leading us toward God.*
—John Ortberg, author of *If You Want To Walk on Water,
You've Got to Get Out of the Boat*